How To Be Smart With Your Part

How To Be Smart With Your Part

A Guide for a Man on the Way Up

Lords A. Leapin

Copyright © 2004 by Lords A. Leapin
Library of Congress Number : 2004105076
ISBN: 1-4134-4046-0

All rights reserved. No part of this book may be reproduced or transmitted in any form or by any means, electronic or mechanical, including photocopying, recording, or by any information storage and retrieval system, without permission in writing from the author.

This book was printed in the United States of America.

Contents

Forward 7

Chapter 1: Which Part are We Talking About? 9
            A discourse to determine the subject matter of
               this book.

Chapter 2: Does It Have Its Own Brain? 21
            An experiment to answer an age-old question.

Chapter 3: Is It Naturally Friendly? 36
            Methods to make your part more friendly to others.

Chapter 4: Your Part When Drinking! 52
            Dangers to your part that occur primarily when
               binging.

Chapter 5: Shrinkage and Other Complexities 68
            The male ego, safe sex and orgasms.

Chapter 6: Everyday Commuting 84
            Safe sex during rush hour.

Chapter 7: Your Part in Exotic Locations 95
            Sex in topless bars. What about it?

Chapter 8: Your Part and Protective Apparel 111
            More about safety for your part!

Chapter 9: Your Part and Pharmaceuticals 122
            Discussions on drugs!

Chapter 10: The Serious Pages 126
    What you should know about sexually transmitted diseases.

FORWARD

Thanks to the person who named and thus inspired this book. Thanks also to my readers and contributors. You know who you are. To preserve anonymity, the names of any non-fictional characters have been changed.

The following is for entertainment purposes only. Should you happen to glean some useful information from it, even better!

Remember: For a Man on the Way Up, Paranoia is a Good Thing!

LL

CHAPTER 1

Which Part are We Talking About?

The typical purchaser of this book will pick it up and instantly be smitten with the most relevant question, Which part are we talking about here and why do we need to read a book about it? First of all I would like to make it clear that we are writing this book for a man on the way up. Now this could be in the corporate world or for that matter in any particular chosen field, including, for example construction. The exact field of the reader does not really matter here, so let us not exclude firemen or the sensitive musician.

What really is important is that the reader has one of these and is interested in learning more about its safety and everyday maintenance.

Now the purchaser is probably thinking cell phones or the always ubiquitous stereo equipment. Even more likely, he may be thinking of the latest desktop computer and whether or not it comes with a DVD player or burner that will make the workday go faster. This is a natural assumption. But no. We are not talking about the kind of part that can be picked up in a typical gadget store like a Radio Shack where you need to buttonhole one of the enlightened audio/

video inventory staff to help you find that perfect cable-connector. This part cannot be directly found on the shelves in an auto-parts store next to the radiator hoses or cans of synthetic motor oil. (Although lubrication can be helpful at times.)

No dear reader, we are not writing along those lines at all. As a man on the way up it is important, I think, to narrow down the issues of this book to a much smaller subset. The key word, I think, in the previous sentence is a focus on the gender issue, **"man."**

This is not to require anyone who is a potential reader of this book to be any specific gender. All that is required is a keen interest in the topic matter. It may, for example, be that you know an individual with one of these and would like to be able to offer some sound advice without having first hand experience. If so, this will be the perfect book for you, because it will be filled with everyday examples that will clarify the issues involved. It could be that you heard about an incident involving one of these and wanted to know if the story was fundamentally sound as you heard it. Perhaps you heard the physical description of a particular thing and wondered, if in fact, it could be that much different from another. Or it may be that first hand experience with these has peaked your interest for more knowledge. Even if you find yourself obsessed on the topic I would say, no matter, you're not alone. You have selected the right book and it will provide a large number of examples of proper usage and maintenance. But I digress.

As you may have intuited, the subject matter is not a thing typically subject to purchase and placement on the coffee table for inspection by your acquaintances when you have your spring garden party. The boss will probably not find it appropriate for discussion at work, unless of course, he has one that is known to impress. Then of course he may have to call a special meeting. But in most company (or companies) that doesn't happen. The topic matter in all of its details and nuances is barely acknowledged and is then swept under (or out of) the door with the rest of the winter sludge before a true chance at enlightenment occurs.

Women's groups may meet ad hoc to discuss related issues at times of great stress or perhaps at the weekly tea-social but often this will lead to the release of quite a bit of misinformation. This book attempts to streamline the release of clear, comprehensible and compelling (the three C's) everyday useful data about the item.

There are many questions that exist about this ethereal wonder! Why does it seem to be there at some times and not at others? Does it have its own brain? Is it possible to have more than one? Well, that isn't a common question unless you're in the serpentine world where such an event happens routinely. How big can one get? To answer this question it is important to move back out of the serpentine world and over into hominidae. To this I say, and making that presumption, How big does one need it? This particular question has never been pursued in the academic or medical world and is currently lacking in valid and constructive study. To answer it would require the healthy application of sampling techniques and statistical analysis to a large part of the population. Nonetheless it's a valid question and one that has been asked for endless years since the evolution of anthropoids. Presumably other animals have asked the question too but they've just been less vocal about it.

The study of this question would require that a substantial population of the opposite (female) gender be surveyed and metrically measured. I am told by those who would know that it is difficult to find a sample population that would not struggle against such measurement. Indeed it would be difficult to gather a sampling group without some sort of scientific fee, oh say $20-$30 each to find enough willing subjects.

For those of you who have not thought much on the subject, you may wonder how that population would be acquired. There are several approaches with which one may come up with a sample group. First of all there is the now all-too-common fax machine approach, which to be honest is fairly scatter-gun in nature. It is important to create a one page explanation of the needs and objectives of the study which can be faithfully reproduced using a typically pixel-challenged fax machine. A sample document would be limited in words and use big print to be legible. The layout below might work in this case:

LOOKING FOR FEMALE VOLUNTEERS
TO ENGAGE IN A SCIENTIFIC STUDY ON THE TOPIC OF HOW BIG IS BIG ENOUGH?

REQUIREMENTS:

1) **VOLUNTEERS MUST BE OVER THE AGE OF CONSENT**
2) **BE WILLING TO ENGAGE IN SPIRITED ROUND-TABLE DISCUSSIONS OF PERSONAL EXPERIENCES AND FEELINGS.**
3) **BE WILLING TO BE METRICALLY MEASURED WITH SCIENTIFICALLY DESIGNED THING-O-METERS.**

VOLUNTEERS WILL BE PAID A FEE OF $25.

PLEASE CALL XXX-XXX-XXX.

This fax would then be released by one of the commercial fax dialers from which we often receive such helpful notices.

Then the consulting team would need to just sit back and wait for the flock of responses from the world of female accountants, corporate secretaries, actuaries, and financiers to respond to the fax sheets which so conveniently show up in their offices.

One can, of course, use other well-known and successful marketing approaches such as direct mail (very similar except you can add in graphical presentations of the round table discussion with chalk-boarded ideas or a few thing-o-meter photographs); or telephone cold-calls, which although reflective of twenty-first century technology, tend to result in less than receptive discussions with the solicited.

In attempting this telephonic process for similar studies, I've noted that the recipient of the call often spends an inordinate amount of time trying to take down the solicitor's name and address (for reasons unknown). Also the solicitor may receive a large number of crank calls using the *69 return call process.

Finally you might say, What about television advertisements? Experience shows that this process is not so easy to implement as one might think. Network programmers seem to require a large number of preliminary program reviews that for some reason tend to reduce the number of successful advertisements that reach final broadcast. But I digress again.

We were talking about the subject of this book, that is, the part to be smart with. And fully focusing now, we've narrowed it down to a part dealing with specifically the male gender. And this is a part commonly owned by most every member of the male group. Not by purchase, however, but by divine right or by evolution depending on how you personally angle on this question. Now I'm going to be direct here and point out that analysis based on divine intervention doesn't fly well in the world of logical discussion. So you won't hear many arguments relying on that theory from me.

Evolution on the other hand can be useful in discussing a number of issues. Evolution can be helpful in determining the structure and functionality of a number of parts.

If for example, we are discussing the pectoralis, that muscle group which grows over time by the repeated use of that usually male exercise machine, the bench press, we can conclude that in its current functionality, it is primarily useful in attracting the female gender. At least we can't think of too many other uses for it. It does produce that nice V shape that women seem to enjoy.

From an anthropological view of pre-hominid man, it was no doubt useful to protect the body organs when one was forced to beat one's breast to frighten off an opponent. Through repeated beatings it appears any ancient ability to offer succor to little pre-hominids has disappeared.

Even if the underlying functionality of the pectoralis is no longer able to support a milk-providing function, the left and right pecs can, with repeated exercise, be instilled with the discipline to move up and down in alternate beats much like an exotic dancer with tassels attached to her bosoms. It's just that nobody wants to watch.

In contrast, the female gender has retained bosoms over these centuries and for a number of reasons other than the fact that we like them. Given that the male figure was busy removing his own through a process of manly self-flagellation, it was left to the woman to retain her bosoms so that someone was able to successfully procreate. The woman of ancient times had to be much more resilient to survive beyond her child-bearing years. First of all, just contemplation of the mating act was often a near-death experience. Coming full-term with a baby and the consequent birth complications that could occur was likely to result in the unfortunate death of the mother.

But if she was fortunate enough to survive the experience the bosoms would necessarily come into play. Those spigots would provide the complete nurturing of a young hominid for several years until the mother got tired of being tackled by the hungry but larger child. This tackling effect came to be known as "weaning."

Size of the bosoms was doubtlessly important in the attraction of a mate since successful procreation would require the generation of a large amount of milk. This intuitive view of women continued on as late as the 20th century at which time the invention of the milkman demeaned the value of a rubenesque woman.

Truth be known, we're not here to talk about the size of ones pecs. Neither are we here to talk about the development of the opposable thumb or the determination of when on the anthropological tree individuals began to straighten up and walk erectly.

The discussion conducted here is on a much more interesting part that has been the subject of physical, religious and to some degree medical investigation since the beginning of human culture when it was discovered that under certain circumstances this part felt extremely good. When combined with other parts it was learned that both parts could feel very good at the same time. And thus a symbiotic relationship was born between those who had part A and those that had part B. The unexpected result of such relationships during the early part of human civilization was individual C. Nowadays we've learned to *expect* a C (that's a fourth C.)

For those of you who believe we may be talking about the religiously treasured bicep, I'm going to have to tell you that you are wrong. Rubbing one's biceps together will not result in a C no matter how long you do it, and from that perspective it is very safe if you are not looking for a C. A systematic examination of the American Medical Encyclopedia reveals that few diseases can be passed between individuals through casual or even intimate bicep contact. It is suggested, however that if you have shingles on your biceps you not rub them all over someone. Who knows what the hell will happen and they probably will think it's bad luck.

At this point the tongue and ear people are doubtlessly clamoring for attention. The tongue people are quick to point out that tongue A will beget a certain pleasure when it makes contact with tongue B. This is true in many circumstances but not in as many as one might think. Furthermore tongue A meeting tongue B is not likely to result in individual C. So we can quickly see that the tongue is not likely to qualify. This is not to imply that the tongue is not worthy of a complete reference on the topic. (We have to keep the tongue group happy.) Simply put, this is not the place to seek that review. The ear advocates can be said to have even less of an argument. Little more, in fact, than the extremely small collection of bicep enthusiasts.

There would be a much stronger argument if we were to stand the ear and tongue advocates side by side with each other, since placing one's tongue in another's ear can be said to have a certain physical pleasure that qualifies for investigation and discussion. With some flexibility this could have been a book on "How to be Smart with Your Parts." It isn't however. Additionally I would like to note that this activity is not gender specific. Either the male or the female can initiate such action and as I would like to point out this is specifically a book for "a man on the way up." As such, it relates to a part that is generally connected with the male.

This is not to suggest that no female has ever had such a part, but generally when they do there is a certain dysfunction associated with it. Perhaps it is completely dysfunctional and only there for show. Sometimes the part is completely removable and can be attached or detached at will with the proper straps and/or snaps. Occasionally the part is functional but it is accessorized with other parts that would appear to be female in nature, making the individual's whole gender somewhat in question.

The first situation generally occurs when a female simply decides that she would like one of these, elects to go down to the nearest medical emporium, and has an operation done, one that used to be only available for the enlightened Swedish. Now I would like to point out that such a decision usually takes more thinking than a morning cup of tea or a "How do you do?" It is, in fact, worthy of a good deal of thinking before making such a decision because the return trip is quite bumpy and difficult to attain. Moreover, having made one of these decisions can create quite another difficult set of every-day decisions. For example, Which is the proper restroom to use? Will my use of the restroom cause a riot at the mini-mall? Am I unnecessarily drawing attention to myself if I only half complete the process? How much should I spend on the new wardrobe? These are not minor questions such as one lump or two!

For those accustomed to using the detachable part, more often than not there is a certain lifestyle accommodation that is going on. The female in question does not believe that she is essentially male as in the prior case, but instead simply wants to be treated as one. Especially during the period in which she is hot and bothered. Thus the apparatus becomes temporary and can be snapped on or snapped off with a clap of the hands (or at least with the release of the proper restraining straps.) The rest of the time the part is not worn. For example it is not worn during the everyday job as a legal secretary. The protrusion is highly likely to be noticed while walking back and forth to the fax machine or water cooler. Moreover it is likely to create a certain amount of intra-office conversation amongst other employees who notice and are forced to speculate on the nature of the pointy object sprouting from the lady's slacks or skirt. Conversationally it is difficult to discuss everyday work matters with a lady wearing one of these since there is a natural tendency to focus all of one's attention on it.

The third situation is doubtlessly the rarest of all. The female possessing a functional version of one of these will almost by definition also possess a functional version of the contrasting part. This results in a major amount of gender confusion throughout almost the whole life of the individual unless one or other of the parts is modified to be less influential in the daily running of the body. This situation is not often advertised by the individual facing it, since it might cause a certain discomfort level for the employees with whom he/she tends to associate. Certainly this also puts a damper on the dating situation. Neither individual would be certain exactly who was getting to third base, but when they got there it would be more complex than usual! It is more normal for the person facing this situation to set up a meeting or date using an intermediary service in which it is possible to disclose such issues prior to actually meeting the other person. This might typically be done by that modern day information superhighway, the internet.

One need simply put an ad in the personals (you know, female searching for male or whatever); address the population of prospective mates by putting in your age preferences; tell a little bit about your background; put in a clear or perhaps slightly blurry picture of yourself depending on your level of self-confidence; and then at the end put in the "Oh By the Way" comment. That is, oh by the way, you happen to have more than your fair share of these types of things. However you are not going to let that stop you from engaging in your fair share of happiness. And being honest about it why should it? Who knows, find the right person and there's no telling what you can do with all of that apparatus!

Now one must use a little discretion in writing and/or answering ads found on the superhighway. It's actually quite a bit like hitchhiking. You take your chances when you get in the cab of that eighteen-wheeler and you take your chances when you do the preliminary investigation of your new and exciting date by exchanging data bits and bytes through a thin copper wire. The descriptive information received by this method from the six foot two former football player who is working as an investment banker at a prominent financial institution in New York may not match up with the actual sender, a five foot three balding auto-mechanic using the hair swirl technique to cover all sides of his head.

It is suggested therefore that you establish the initial meeting at a fairly populated restaurant or location where you would likely draw attention if your date suddenly placed a gag in your mouth and started dragging you to his SUV. Of course it may be that this dating technique is actually exciting for you. It might be smart nonetheless to have a cover individual (that is, someone who knows your purpose and concerns) attend the same restaurant and covertly keep an eye on the person at hand. She can warn you if, for example, when you leave the dining area to use the ladies room the new beau crawls around the table and sniffs the chair seat.

Perhaps it's time to get back on topic. This is, of course, a book that tells a man on the way up how to be smart with his part.

Sniffing. I'm going to talk about sniffing in public for just a moment before we move on. As a general principle, public sniffing is generally not construed to be sophisticated person-to-person behavior. Let me give an example. I recall in one of my former lives, that I would amuse myself at times by doing card and other minor sleight of hand tricks on my daily commuter train. I learned countless ways to have someone select a card so that I could find it in some amazing fashion. Usually this would elicit verbal reviews such as "How did you do that?" "How did that card get in my shoe?" "How did that card get in my purse?" "How did that card get in my bra?" (a good trick—that).

One time I decided on a different variation of finding the selected card, one in which I would leave it in the deck, but use the assistance of my beautiful victim to find it. So she carefully selects a card ensuring that it is, in fact, the card meant for her; looks at it; replaces it in the deck; and looks at me with her lovely dark eyes matching her long brunette tresses. I peer back into those eyes, then gently grasp her hand and slowly pull it up to my nose. Whereupon, I proceed to overtly sniff it, much like a French pig searching for truffles. (There are of course no oinking sounds.)

It was then that I noticed my beautiful subject had a minor look of shock, much as if an alien dripping some thickish fluid had stepped out of an oblong aircraft nearby. But I presumed it was my imagination and proceeded to fan the cards and then sniff each one until I reached the card that had been so lovingly selected. Having become accustomed to verbal feedback at the end of each trick, it took me by surprise when upon revealing the card, she declined to comment either positively or negatively but simply got out of the seat and moved away. It was at that moment that I learned the negative power of sniffing.

With the possible exception of a woman who has recently put on some fragrant concoction purchased in an upscale department store, most individuals will take a certain offense if you appear to be sniffing them in order to track or identify them. The implication is that they smell enough to be identified, which in modern-day society is generally taboo. (This is not, of course, always the case, such as the Orinoo Indians living in the Brazilian rainforest where certain smells are determined to be useful in identification.)

What's the bottom line here? You will not endear yourself to the opposite sex if you appear to be sniffing them.

I could go on here with other public taboos but some of them don't really need a lot of explanation. Common sense should apply. Don't for example talk so vociferously that you spit on people. How many times has that happened at cocktail hour when the person talking to you has downed several beers and then rain starts to fall as you learn about the current downturn in the stock market. Perhaps if it was an upturn people could hold their liquor?

I think I would like to get back on topic again. That is, how to be smart with your part. After a certain mental rumination of the previous pages you are probably hypothesizing exactly what part it is that that can engender such direct and indirect thought processes related to life in general. No doubt you are thinking it has to be something fairly important to the male gender of the species. You are on track here!

I think a large portion of the readers at this point have probably narrowed it down to two or three specific parts. But at this point I'm going to make it even easier for you.

Thinking back to one of my earlier life events on this general topic matter, I recall that there was an article that I read in the sixth grade in a men's magazine (I really had no business reading this) that detailed the injustices of some men to other men. The article described the capture of one man by others in the Ku Klux Klan and the unfortunate removal of his scrotum. I was quite taken aback and disturbed by this article. In my book report the next day I described the article in class and ended the report with the factual statement that they removed his scrotum.

At that point, and in front of the class, I turned to my teacher and asked the question, What is a scrotum? My sixth grade teacher thought about it for a second and then thoughtfully replied, "It's a muscle in your leg."

Years later I am thankful that my teacher had the foresight to sidestep that body part so successfully. I too am going to sidestep that body part and tell you directly that this is not a book about scrotums. And thank heavens for that! Can you imagine reading a whole book about balls?

I think not. There has to be more meat to the story than that. Although it could be said that there is a lot of literature that would be supportive of the importance of balls in attaining one's objectives in life, that's not the part of importance here. No. It's quite close to the scrotum however. So close that you might think they are connected. And they are! Yes dear reader (and I hope you weren't guessing rectum), the part that we are following quite closely in this book is the male penis.

It goes by many other names that you may have heard, such as Missile, Whanger, Whacker, Gonzo, Willie, Torpedo, Thingy, Bart, Dick, Little Joe, Rocket, The Pipe, Schlong, One-Eyed Wonder Snake, but is best known, of course, as The Artful Dodger.

Now that we've established the subject of our book you can sit back and read without the natural tension that comes with suspense.

CHAPTER 2

Does It Have Its Own Brain?

Many individuals of the gentler sex have asked the question in all naiveté, Does it have its own brain? To answer that difficult question one must utilize objective observation and then apply the deductive reasoning of a Sherlock Holmes. Even then one may not come away with a fully satisfactory answer. Since this is an answer book we will try, however.

To do so, we will examine it from three perspectives.

1) Can we see a brain under physical examination?
2) What is its psychology under certain situations?
3) Is its activity always in accordance with the more popular cranial brain?

Can we see a brain under physical examination?

In order to answer this question we conducted a scientific examination in a similar fashion to that described in the introductory chapter. Following the aforementioned method, we prepared a fax requesting a wide sample population and sent it to the broad population of fax machines near the San Francisco area in the great state of flexibility.

LOOKING FOR MALE VOLUNTEERS
TO ENGAGE IN A SCIENTIFIC STUDY ON THE TOPIC OF DOES IT HAVE ITS OWN BRAIN?

REQUIREMENTS:

1) **VOLUNTEERS MUST BE OVER THE AGE OF CONSENT.**
2) **BE WILLING TO ENGAGE IN SPIRITED ROUND-TABLE DISCUSSIONS OF PERSONAL EXPERIENCES AND FEELINGS.**
3) **BE WILLING TO HAVE YOUR THINGY PHYSICALLY EXAMINED AND STUDIED BY QUALIFIED MEDICAL PRACTITIONERS.**

VOLUNTEERS WILL BE PAID A FEE OF $25.

PLEASE CALL XXX-XXX-XXX.

Since we had found, from previous experience, that telephonic response could enable certain cranks to call back and tie up the line, we decided to simply put an answering machine at the call-in number summarizing the study and providing the address where interested parties should meet on the following Monday. The fee, of course, was to ensure that we received a large enough sample to create a statistically valid study that would be unbiased in all aspects. On Monday morning we quickly learned that our planning of this medical study was deficient in some manner.

As I approached our temporary clinic with my two assistants Lana and Tommy, we expected to be met by a few medical technicians to assist us for the day. Instead, we found a large and rather boisterous crowd of men between the ages of 20 and 40 who seemed to be clamoring near the entrance. As we pushed our way through the crowd it seemed to close around us leaving almost no avenue with which to carry our supplies. After making our way into the waiting room, we immediately shut the door to gather some breathing room and provide ourselves with time for stratagems.

We quickly determined that if we opened the door and let in a large number of the crowd we would find ourselves under a siege that would be incompatible with the objectives of our plan. So we decided to let in 10 men at a time and then lock the door until we could ensure a calm stability within the clinic premises. Admittedly we are not overly financed and in the clinical examination room, only had 10 usable gurneys. We had more seats in the observation/discussion room that would be available if needed, but given that there were only the three of us (plus technicians), it seemed that for the moment we should postpone inviting more of these rather loud men inside.

Initially we set up two lines for admittance with Tommy and Lana tag-teaming to register the sample population and ensure they met the basic requirements of the study. Naturally they had to provide some government-issued photo identification that would ensure they were over the age of 21 and be willing to talk in relatively intimate terms about their personal member and its activities. We wanted to weed out the crowd that wanted to be paid $25 just for having one.

Having initially qualified the group, we herded them back into the examination room and assigned each a cot to sit on. Now as the time came for Lana and Tommy to give each of their subject's thingy an examination, we were surprised to find that when the first two examinees were asked to lower their trousers, like a reverberation, the other eight individuals in the room did the same without being asked. It was a little unnerving to have so many individuals demonstrate a lack of inhibition with the disrobing process.

Then a second anomaly occurred. As Lana requested her patient to extend himself for basic examination and measurement (using a metric ruler of course) he seemed to have little concern with the examination and did not seem to find it particularly stimulating. Lana, as a practical matter, is rather attractive. (I would note here that not only our first patient but most of the other individuals examined on this day had thingys that were greater than the often quoted average figure of 15.24 centimeters (or six inches) by the way. I will remark on this later.)

In contrast, when Tommy pulled out his ruler for the same measurement, his patient's thingy suddenly became erect. Tommy turned at me with a questioning look in his eyes, and then suddenly the entire room was flooded with excited penises wildly waving in the air. Tommy and Lana stepped back from their patients and we looked at each other. We all were thinking the same thing. These thingys were talking to each other! They appeared to be conversing. Now one might assume that this is a complete impossibility, but rather than doubt ourselves we continued the investigation.

Medically we then injected each of our sample population with radioactive dye and then, one after another, walked each to the mini-MRI/MRA. At this unique, one-of-a-kind designed station, each subject was placed into the machine and then a special thingy-isolation-device was strapped on to the subject's member to record in detail its inner structure. Upon completion, the magnetic resonance machine was turned on to produce a detailed cross-sectional physical examination that was printed for review and analysis by our paid specialist. From an internal (and somewhat cursory perspective,) and this was repeated over and over again throughout the day, our MRI/MRA specialist was unable to conclusively state that she had found any internal semblance of a brain within the male penis.

Yet as she jotted down over and over again in her notes, each of the male members she examined appeared to have a head. Although some of them had a foreskin which tended to camouflage the fact, if you pulled it back it had a head! Objectively we were left with the thought that it seemed unlikely that there could be a head without a brain. Especially when we were able to see them conversing while their owners remained relatively silent!

What is its psychology?

Now we wanted to preclude the possibility that our study subjects were actually communicating though some other method such as hand signals or eye contact. It was important for our experiment to prove that the communication occurring was independent of the signals sent by the large brain sitting in each person's (regular) head.

So we briefly pulled everyone off their gurneys to scientifically examine this question.

First, we moved everyone to the side of the room, without telling each subject the purpose of our next experiment. As they waited, it appeared their members were no longer communicating. We then randomly selected the first of our disrobed patients and placed a large paper bag over his head, much like you would receive if you bought a turkey at the nearby grocery-mart. This paper bag would act to block all normal communication channels that would be operative through the primary brain. We then walked the now incommunicado subject over to one of the gurneys and sat him down. Next we took a second subject; placed a bag on his head; and sat him on the gurney next to the first. We continued this experiment amongst all of our patients but we had barely gotten to the third when it became apparent that the members of our first two subjects had begun to communicate again without the aid of the primary brain. Soon *all of the thingys* were again excitedly conversing with each other without the aid of the primary brain. This was major evidence indeed about the existence of a second brain.

Then, almost as an afterthought, we decided to see if the conversations would continue if we took tiny bags and placed them on the heads of our subjects' members. Unfortunately we lacked extremely tiny bags so we utilized paper sandwich bags, which at first tended to fall off due to their wide shape. To solve this problem we twisted the bags to make them thinner and then secured them tightly around the thingys with supermarket fruit-bag twisties. At first, it looked like the communications would continue but within a minute or two all activity amongst the members appeared to cease. We were staggered by the implications here. Both the upper and lower brains appeared to have the ability to communicate and to have sensory capabilities that could be blocked.

We then removed the bags from both heads of each of our scientific subjects, (who I must admit looked a little wild-eyed at this time) and led them into the team room for discussions on the topic.

Lana was our discussion team leader in charge of the conversational feedback to be gleaned. In addition she kept track of responses on a chalk-board as she encouraged individuals to provide input to our experiment.

(I would like to point out, before we go any further, that the individuals included in our study group seemed to be unusually outgoing in their dress. Black leather seemed to be the predominant style for some reason, despite the fact of the relatively warm

California climate. This may explain why the group seemed to warm up to the discussion, as there was this commonality among them that led to a certain group "vibe.")

Does it act in accordance with the cranial brain?

The purpose of our team-related exercise was to determine if there was a dichotomy of operation that occurred between the upper and lower brain. And if so, when did one take over for the other?

Lana introduced the topic as a hypothetical story that had been heard many times from individuals of the female persuasion. As the story goes, a typical relationship would build over a period of time between a woman and her male friend. (There seemed to be some confusion over this simple parable as the men in the room seemed to make eye contact a lot here.) As the relationship would continue, the relationship would get stronger, resulting in more time spent together, a growing level of common interests, an increase in the group of common friends with a resultant tighter bond. Although over time this bond would become quite strong, at some point the male of the twosome would find himself in an indiscretion, a dalliance with another individual of the opposite sex (once again some eye-contact confusion here.)

Lana continued with her recounting of the hypothetical. The common explanation heard from a large number of women who experienced this phenomena was that the male in the relationship was "letting his penis do his thinking for him."

Having made this statement Lana posed the question to the team group. "I would like you to relate yourselves to the male in this situation and respond by putting yourself in his place. Have you at times felt that your sexual actions have not reflected the *common-sense* thoughts that you have experienced at the same moment?"

It appeared that the apparent confusion associated with the group was resolved fairly easily at this point due to the number of hands that went up to answer the question. As bluntly noted by one particularly fashionable dresser (Loni) wearing a faux bullet bandolier over his shoulder, "There have been many times in my life when my head told me to do one thing and Little Loni told me to do another." Little Loni is, of course, another name to add to the pre-determined list from chapter one.

This concept was echoed over and over again by the men not only in our first group but those that came after. They confirmed that actions taken by the body were often different from those suggested by the traditional brain.

And the concerns generated by this independent penile thought process were extensive for our sample groups. Many of our patients seemed wrought with regret that their penile brain was able to overrule its cranial partner, typically resulting in a sexual encounter that shouldn't have happened. These regrets fell into several categories:

It wasn't a relationship, it was a one-night stand. Actually it appeared that oftentimes this could have been stated as: It wasn't a relationship, it was a 15 minute stand. A large number of these individuals appeared to remain with their partner for under 15 minutes, ruling out a psychologically fulfilling relationship.

I shouldn't have done what it told me to do! The common sense cranial brain appears to be the smarter but perhaps weaker brother at certain times. In the late 20th century, a large number of 15 minute sexual encounters with different partners has been determined to be unsafe. Too many little gremlins that float around in the bloodstream can have a devastating impact on the ability of a person's body to maintain life. (More on this later as we discuss strategies to avoid these gremlins under different circumstances, on the train, in the air, etc.)

I told him/her I wouldn't see him/her again, but I did. This is an age-old story about dumping or being dumped in a relationship. It's an issue you can spend many hours on a psychiatrist's couch to discuss. Now, one can spend money on session after session of analysis but let's cut to the chase. Just get over it and move on! The relationship is over! Sorry about that. I just got a little perturbed.

I didn't want to be alone. OK. So you couldn't go to a movie and sit in a big audience and feel a part of the crowd. Many individuals have survived alone throughout history. Take Jerimiah Johnson and Robinson Crusoe as examples. Get a bear or a puppet as a friend for god's sake!

Having identified these concerns, we wanted to further determine what was the "enabler" which would result in the dominance of the lower brain. So we asked the sample group to explain the circumstances when the lower brain tended to take control. We requested that the responses be based on anecdotal events for which the population had specific remembrance. After passing out the surveys and reading back the situations that occurred, we decided to group the enablers by category.

Enabler #1: Alcohol

It seems that the generous application of alcohol on a given evening could switch *off* the cranial brain while switching *on* the penile brain. Unfortunately, while making the brain transition, at the same time it appears that the actual dexterity of the member becomes a little less efficient. It doesn't work as well. It reminds one of a boxer who has been put in the ring in the 5th round. He comes out fighting but he's a little punch drunk. So he misses a lot of shots.

Enabler #2: Drugs

Like alcohol but at a more extreme level, drugs appear to turn off the cranial brain resulting in direction from below. Depending on the drug du jour, the instructions from below may be less or completely ineffective.

Enabler # 3 Loneliness

OK. Perhaps this is getting a little depressing now so let's not dwell here.

Enabler #4 Hormones

Yes. Sometimes you just get in the mood to let the lower brain take control. This is seen in adults but is more prominent in adolescents (known as raging hormones.)

Enabler #5 Good Communications

I think we've all seen this. Some individuals are very good communicators with potential sexual partners (or at least have a good line) and somehow this communication skill, which perhaps requires all of the attention of the upper brain, allows the lower brain to take over the remaining functions. Whereas the previously named enablers tend to be viewed in a negative fashion, often men on the way up with Enabler #5 are looked upon as heroes by society.

To focus now and summarize what we found from our little experiment, physically our medical examiner was unable to physically see a penile brain through the use of modern MRI/ MRA medical equipment. Instead she was able to see cross-section functional components used primarily for urinary and reproductive functions. Nonetheless as she summarized her intimate view of several hundred male members, "It sure looks like they've got heads." And where there are heads, oftentimes there are brains.

Our psychological examination led us to somewhat startling observations. Under certain situations the male members became quite communicative, waving and twitching at each other in certain, secretive, cultural patterns. We were not able to determine precisely what they were saying but it is possible that we could learn, given enough time and candid observation. Naturally, if we were to engage in a more time-consuming and dedicated study, there is a chance we would contaminate the sample group itself, resulting in unwanted consequences. (Like inadvertently teaching primitive tribes to smoke by studying them while holding a cigarette in your hand.) Because of this anthropological study risk, we decided to draw conclusions from the data at hand rather than extend the study and accidentally affect the male member psychology or culture.

We demonstrated that inter-member communications of the male thingy could continue without the benefit of the upper cranial brain through the use of our bag experiment.

Now if you are a research experiment purist, you might wonder, Why did we have to go to these lengths? Couldn't we just duplicate this experiment through the use of the more commonly used white rats?

Well I would like to point out that it is hard enough to get grocery bags that will fit both human heads and the male member. Can you imagine how difficult our experiments would have been if we had first had to cover the rat's head with a tiny bag and then cover his thingy with an even smaller one? Hygienic requirements (we can only use them once) would have forced us to enter into an expensive agreement with bag manufacturers to make tiny rat-head bags and tiny thingy bags. Clearly this would have increased our expenses beyond what could be funded with our meager budget.

Perhaps you might wonder, What about rhesus monkeys? Have you ever looked at one? They look like they might have a lot of interest in this kind of topic! Although clearly our bag budget would have been lower with rhesus monkeys, we still would have been faced with other problems when we surveyed them for their anecdotal experiences of upper to lower brain transitions. We have no way to translate their discussions of previous life experiences.

No, the best thing we could do here was take an objective sample of the male population from a major SMSA (Standard Metropolitan Statistical Area) and get real-life feedback.

For all of you nay-sayers I challenge you to collect enough rhesus monkeys and find the correct size of head-bags! But let's continue.

We found that physical evidence of a tiny brain could not be seen and yet the psychology and activities of the male member suggest that one is there. As famed detective Sherlock Holmes once suggested, when you have eliminated all of the other possibilities, what remains must be the answer. Another way this has been stated is "If it walks like a duck and quacks like a duck, we must conclude it is a duck."

If this is so, where is the mysterious brain that steps forward to control the penis at certain times? Why are we unable to discern it through normal analytical techniques? The answer is somewhat intuitive. We can hypothesize that the brain cannot be seen because it exists at a tiny, near molecular level. In fact, since we know that no visible organ can be seen we can deduce that perhaps it exists as a tiny hive-like intelligence where the accumulated knowledge is transmitted back and forth. Yes, as you may have surmised, the lower brain is the cumulative knowledge of all the little guys swimming back and forth in the vas deferens, the spermatozoa. And this (at least partially) explains why control tends to shift back and forth between the upper and lower brain. That is, concurrent with sexual activity, a large portion of the male's brains are released from the male's body, enabling the cranial brain to easily re-takeover. (This hypothesis is referred to as the "Unified Theory of the Male Brain.")

We noticed the actual workings of this theory as each sample group transitioned through the survey stage and then was asked to leave through the rear of the clinic. It appeared the large amount of communication that occurred during the team-building process resulted in a lot of enabling. We noted that a lot of the men (even amongst themselves I might add) found it necessary to shed themselves of some brains prior to leaving the premises. This was not particularly helpful to us since it presented some distraction to the individuals coming into the front office for registration and may possibly have distracted/biased results of subsequent groups.

In an additional note, we found that some of the sample group that came in early in the morning found it necessary to return to the clinic approximately five or six hours later. They seemed to feel that we might wish to interview them again (and of course pay them their fee which I must admit we were quickly running low on.) And we didn't catch on immediately, letting two or three go through completely before we noticed the deception. Although we had to discard their compiled results from the second time through, we did notice that they elected to shed brains again during the second pass. This clearly demonstrated the ability of males to recover and lose their brains again over a five to six hour period. This brain recovery ability doubtless requires more study, since the minimal recovery time would be somewhat less than demonstrated and our sample in this case of a few individuals was very small. To better understand this recovery period, we would of necessity need to design a more focused experiment.

Seeing as how this brain-shedding process is actually very pleasurable, it becomes important that a man on the way up strikes a certain balance of not too many and not too few times to regenerate his brains in a given period. If one is constantly reducing one's intelligence by, say doing it twice a day, pretty soon there won't be much natural intelligence left. We have noted this behavior primarily in the adolescent world (thus resulting in adolescent behavior.) However it is not restricted there. Many adults find themselves shedding brains much too often. We don't want to say however that there is a specific defined amount that should occur. Some individuals seem to operate better given the freedom to expel excess brains on a regular basis.

On the other side we have individuals whose brains become worn out and need to be replaced more often, therapeutically if for no other reason. If done infrequently enough, this brain refreshment process may begin to fail. At a certain stage we must become aware of the adage, "Use it or lose it." So a balance needs to be established for a man in for the long-haul.

How best should that balance be determined you ask? This is not an easy question. And the answer will differ depending on the individual. Perhaps a guideline can be established by observing the activities of other individuals identified as "typical." And occupation can be a guiding factor. If we look at lawyers for example, shedding one's brains for renewal purposes is not particularly important. The old ones will generally do just fine. So perhaps once every several weeks should be adequate. Sports figures, on the other hand, typically find brain renewal to be a very important part of their lives. Perhaps it keeps the metabolism flowing that is necessary to create lean muscle mass. From what we can observe regarding professional basketball and football players, it is not unusual for these figures to shed brains at least once a day if not more. Oftentimes they must find partners to help them keep up such a rigorous schedule.

Although these are only relative guidelines of frequency, we have prepared a short list of occupations based on observation. These statistics can help determine an appropriate brain shedding schedule:

FREQUENCY OF BRAIN RENEWAL BY OCCUPATION

OCCUPATION	NUMBER OF TIMES PER MONTH
SPORTS FIGURE/ROCK STAR	40
PRESIDENT OF USA*	30
INVESTMENT BANKER	25
CONSTRUCTION WORKER	12
ACCOUNTANT	10
DOCTOR	6
POSTMAN	4
ACTUARY	3
LAWYER	1
RELIGIOUS FANATIC	0

*Can vary dramatically.

The dramatic importance of brain renewal can easily been seen in our first three occupations, Sports Figure/Rock Star, President of the USA, and Investment Bankers. These combined groups tend to dominate the other occupational categories. The necessity for renewal drops off significantly as we move into the categories of construction worker, accountant and doctor. Moving further down the list, renewal is less necessary for the postman, actuary and, of course, lawyers. Finally, there is absolutely no need for brain renewal with religious fanatics. They seldom use any of their natural intelligence.

Although it is not altogether necessary to have a partner to accomplish these frequencies, it is often helpful. Auto-stimulation can become somewhat tiring after a number of repeated episodes. If one uses foresight, it is possible to find a more compatible partner based on her specific ability to provide aid. Given the frequencies required by a number of these male occupations, we thought it would be helpful to provide a similar chart of observed potential partners for compatibility purposes.

COMPATIBLE PARTNERS TO AID IN
THE BRAIN RENEWAL PROCESS

OCCUPATION	NUMBER OF TIMES PER MONTH
SPORTS FIGURE/ROCK STAR GROUPIE	40
WHITE HOUSE INTERN*	30
CHEERLEADER	25
WAITRESS	12
EXECUTIVE ASSISTANT	10
NURSE	6
HOUSEWIFE	4
SUPER MODEL	3
LEGAL SECRETARY	1
RELIGIOUS FANATIC (FEMALE)	0

*Can vary dramatically.

Heading the list of renewal aid occupations are the particularly capable Sports Figure/Rock Star Groupie, White House Intern, and Cheerleader. These occupations have demonstrated over and over their ability to provide support for their male counterparts. In the mid-level occupations we have Waitress, Executive Assistant and the somewhat underrated Nurse. Nurses, we find, can at times rise further on the list to approach the cheerleader level but it is a spotty record. Without a doubt they do have their moments. At the lower end we have Housewives, Super Models (who really don't have to support anyone) and the popular but all-too-focused on their work Legal Secretaries. Once again at the lowest level we have religious fanatics (who just don't get it.)

Given the necessity for brain renewal for certain individuals and the amount of time spent in contemporary travel we are able to predict with some accuracy the nature of the vehicles that will be suitable for transportation. Those individuals in the upper third frequency group will tend toward Large Limousines and SUVs. The frequency requirements for busy individuals ensure that they must take this into account when making an automotive purchase. Those in the second group will generally tend to own mid-size sedans or coupes given the reduced need for a vehicle with reclining space. Within the lower third, (not including Religious Fanatics) we have an exception in that the Super Model will typically have a Larger Car or Limousine simply because they need to find vehicles worthy of the excess cash they have available. However other categories in the lower third will tend toward the smaller vehicles, such as the VW or newly popular Mini-Cooper. Finally, many religious fanatics will find a bicycle or mo-ped suitable for most day-to-day travel. There are, of course, many exceptions to these lists. They should not be construed to be the only vehicle selections that can be made by individuals in these occupations. Moreover, we admit the study used to determine these selections could be improved by increasing the sample size.

How To Be Smart With Your Part

BRAIN RENEWAL REQUIREMENTS PER MONTH

TYPICAL VEHICLE	NUMBER OF TIMES PER MONTH	EXCEPTIONS
LARGE LIMOUSINE/SUV	40	
LARGE LIMOUSINE/SUV	30	
LARGE LIMOUSINE/SUV	25	
MID-SIZE SEDAN/COUPE	12	
MID-SIZE SEDAN/COUPE	10	
MID-SIZE SEDAN/COUPE	6	
VW/MINI COOPER	4	
VW/MINI COOPER	3	Super Model Exception/ Large Limo/SUV
VW/MINI COOPER	1	
BICYCLE	0	Religious Fanatic Exception/ Occasional Jumbo Jet

Thus we can suggest that if a man on the way up would like to be efficiently smart with his part, he should do a little up-front planning. And I think we have a little of the chicken or egg first problem here, but if one knows the occupation he is planning to enter it will be helpful in determining the amount of brain renewal that will be required. Similarly if he is looking to connect up with the gentler gender, it will enable him to hone down the dating dilemma and focus on getting dates from women in the occupations that will appropriately support his brain renewal cycle. Finally, if we broaden the parameters to which this data can be applied, our observations can aid in the selection of appropriate vehicles to support your specific requirements. Remember, the average male gets in and out of a car 4-6 times a day. That's a lot of time spent in a car, oftentimes alone, but oftentimes not.

CHAPTER 3

Is It Naturally Friendly?

Many women have noted that on certain occasions, slow dancing for instance, that the male organ seems to want to join in with a dance of its own. It just shows up, when it could have simply remained hidden and unassuming. Your male partner is gliding you back and forth to the sounds of your favorite mood music. You're feeling rather comfortable and serene in his arms, and all of a sudden you have an extra acquaintance trying to make his presence known. And in a most sensitive place! Coincidence? I think not. It appears that it can happen anywhere, not just at private times. It is commonplace to have it happen in the middle of a wedding reception. Where is the propriety? What is its motivation?

It is easy to develop a number of conspiracy theories here. Perhaps it acts as a pickpocket's distraction making it easy to slip off a valuable trinket while stuffing it casually in one's back pocket. If so, it would be a valuable skill to add to a cut-purse's repertoire.

Perhaps it is merely fabric of the imagination . . . a sensitivity that exists only in the minds of some women who come in contact with the male gender. Could it be that with sufficient analysis we could disprove the existence of the all-too-apparent male tool?

Hypothetically it might be that the woman in question simply is physically so sensitive in her own private area that she feels a swelling that doesn't exist.

Nah!

She was right in the first place.

The male penis is, in fact, a very social animal. Just like the casual relationships struck on a more broad-based human level, the penis is naturally friendly. Unlike the cranial brain that passes much of its information through spoken channels, the male member, must by nature, communicate its desires indirectly by sign language and by touch. There's no mouthful of 30-odd teeth that can tell his favorite squeeze that he would like to see her! Instead, the closest he can do to make contact is ensure she notices him!

How best to do that except by standing up and saluting during the parade! The number of alternative methods and opportunities for a member to show his attention and say hello is relatively limited. Many of them would be considered to be in poor taste for Western (and most other) cultures.

Alternative #1: The cat approach

Say you're a guy in a liquor store purchasing a bottle of champagne for a party to be attended later in the evening. You've been spending your time trying to determine if the sparkling wine that costs $8 is really the same (just another name) as a bottle of champagne that costs $30. You're too proud to ask the sales clerk who might laugh at you and think (moron!)

Out of the corner of your eye, a beautiful woman in a short business skirt and blouse with two unclasped buttons leans down at the display next to you and selects a mid-priced champagne and holds it in front for inspection. She tells you that she too is going to the same party and places the bottle back in order to select another. As she leans over to complete that motion a transition happens. The lower brain kicks into gear but decides that (for whatever reason) the opportunity for brain renewal is not particularly attractive at the moment. Yet the need for attention remains. And the desire to make a mark on the object of his interest becomes paramount.

Thus in the manner of your favorite pet, you remove your now intent member from his normal hiding place and proceed to whiz on the shelved champagne bottles and then on the shoes of the lady in question. Finally to ensure your territory is adequately marked, you now proceed to draw a yellow rectangle around the lady (who is now quite wide-eyed with horror I might add.)

Although this relationship-establishing approach might work adequately in the feline world, there are currently few occasions to use this technique among the human cultures with which I am familiar. First of all there are several downsides to this attention-getting approach.

Downside #1

This isn't the kind of attention your member needs. Rather than attracting a friend of the opposite design, this is more likely to attract a member of the local constabulary. In fact it is recommended that if you engage in this sort of activity, upon finishing your "specification of territory" you immediately run away from it and never return. So right from the get-go it is a self-defeating process.

Downside #2

The female in question will not find you attractive from this action. In fact, just the opposite! Don't just take my word for it. If you are unsure, just take a male cat; position him over one of your female friends; and then squeeze until he pees on her. She will not be amused. Trust me on this one.

Downside #3

Downsides #1 and #2 are more than temporary in nature. They will have lasting power. In other words, if you take this approach to meeting members of the opposite sex, they will not forget. In fact these are things that legends are made of. My recommendation is find a better legend.

Upside: Free Food and Drink in the Slammer.

Alternative #2: Join a puppet show

Another major attention-getter that can be found in certain big cities is somewhat unusual in character. In certain locales and theatrical districts one can join a penis-puppet show. Now this is one way for your member to be certain that it gets a large amount of attention during a relatively short and controlled period of time. One need only work up the act; learn the appropriate lines; create the appropriate mini props; synchronize the actions to the audio; and one can mesmerize an audience for hours on end. The audience may well contain a number of female attendees who will enjoy the "off the wall" humor resulting from such sketches. The more bohemian ladies may well appreciate this somewhat loose approach to entertainment. But once again there are certain downsides. If you find your puppetry is not skilled, try scrotum billiards, painful but effective.

Downside #1
   If not one of the official troupes touring the country, your performance is likely to be anonymous. So you could spend a lot of time twisting and molding your thing but no one will know it was you! You could, of course, clearly advertise your name in the program if not concerned about stepping on someone's copyrighted act!

Downside #2
   The number of penis puppet troupes is fairly limited. And tryouts can be a little intimidating! So if this is your style be prepared to mix and match with the other "members" of the troupe.

Downside #3
   There's not a lot of job security in penis puppets. If you piss-off your producer chances are that you can be replaced rather easily. Unlike movie star faces to which women grow attached, in general, one penis looks like another.

Upside: If you're lucky you'll get an attractive make-up artist to make sure your thingy is blemish-free!

Alternative #3: Engage in a job in which friendly members are a requirement

If your thingy really wants to get noticed, consider a job as a male-exotic dancer. It may be a cliché, but it rings true. When a male dancer steps down off that stage and into that audience of screaming women, his pocket rocket is going to have a lot of opportunities to directly shake hands with his adoring crowd. If there is a double standard in the world of entertainment this is it! Women participating in this close-up form of entertainment are given the go-ahead to do what they want within the limit of the dancer's patience or desire. If he has selected that method of making cash, it stands to reason that neither he nor his member is going to become upset over a woman's efforts to demonstrate her (often drunken) desire to become friendly on extremely short notice.

Downside #1

If not pursued on a full-time basis, this job only works well in combination with certain other professions. Since this is a book for a man on the way up, it may not apply long-term for individuals in the exotic dance profession. First of all, there aren't many promotions that will occur. This is basically a real-time cash compensation business. (In fact much of the cash is under the table.) So except for the obvious relationship advantages, don't expect many occupational enhancements over time. We are all aging!

So what job combinations work well here? The "I'm still in college and just making cash to pay my bills" profession works well and may generate extra tips. It certainly works for women in the same profession! The blue-collar construction guy who is shaking his thing for the fun of it may do well here. What about the white-collar guy who works in the marketing department during the day, forecasting the need to manufacture more computer chips? Here there may be a problem. Imagine yourself two hours after giving an important presentation to your marketing vice president (Mrs. Willis) on the number of PC sales that will drive profitability to your chip manufacturing firm. She was impressed by your command of the demographic trends and has asked follow-up questions in order to more carefully build a business case for top management. You know that you've impressed her and can expect some positive feedback.

At six you leave your day job to pursue that extra cash and friendly environment for your favorite appendage. You drive several blocks to the party side of town where you have been hired as part of the evening entertainment at the local club (which is partial to attracting women on the prowl.) After changing into your first costume as "Baseball Buddy," you hear the introduction of the MC and stroll out on stage to the salsa beat of "Take me out to the ball game" gyrating and jumping while thrusting out your "bat" to best advantage.

As you move amongst the vocal group of women who are waiting your intimate arrival, they stuff ones and fives down the minor piece of cloth (jock floss) that remains as cover-up from your baseball uniform. Then as you turn to move into that last row of excited women you see "Mrs. Willis!!!"

You have now reached a turning point in your marketing career. Which way it turns is not particularly clear, however it's going to be a bumpy road regardless!!

Downside #2

Once again, the number of these troupes is limited.

Downside #3

This alternative is limited to those of us with tight abs, who stay in shape. Bald men on the way up need not apply here. Although a toupee may seem like a reasonable method of rearranging genetics, most women can see through such artifices. Think about it. They've been taught to apply makeup since their pre-teens. If you're going to fool anyone with your toupee it's probably other men. So what's the point?

For those with a potbelly in their early twenties, don't try to fool yourself into thinking that you can shake your booty to the delight of everyone in attendance. You'll just be shaking your confidence. Can you remember the last time you walked into a gentlemen's bar and didn't hear someone comment on the dancer that didn't quite measure up to the expected standard.

Why subject yourself to embarrassment for the small number of dollars you can expect to receive?

There is an exception here. If your thingy is extremely talented on its own, say nine or more inches in length, all other appearance related issues may become irrelevant. In that event simply sign yourself up and awe the crowd.

Upside: This can actually become a well-paying gig. You need only join up with a group of similar-minded individuals with good advertising and it may become a regular party at the local bar of choice. Once those dollars start flowing there's no telling where it will end. And you're getting paid to be friendly, a natural state of your thingy as we have noted before.

You get to meet a lot (a whole lot) of at least temporarily interested females. This frenzied level of female interest will occur in almost no occupations other than President of the United States, Rock Star, and Prominent Sports Athlete.

This may be one of the best ways for your thingy to make an unusual number of friends.

Alternative #4 Attend a nudist colony

In principle this sounds like a good way for your appendage to meet like-minded opposites. You simply go to the nearest hedonistic beach, remove all restrictive clothing, and dangle in the wind while drinking a frozen daiquiri with a little umbrella balanced on the edge of your glass. If you're lucky you won't even have to search out the bartender on the beach. The attractive waitress will come sand-hopping over the dunes wearing nothing but a smile and carrying an order-pad.

Downside #1

Yes it sounds good but the practice isn't quite as enticing as one might expect. First of all, the number of beautiful people attending nudist colonies is a relatively small percentage of the total. Imagine instead a large number of male and female individuals with extra weight on their hips beached on the sand and unable to move without causing minor tremors in the local tectonic faults.

You may find a few slim sun worshippers who don't mind being worshipped, however they will likely be surrounded by a large number of 65 year-old balding sea lions. You aren't likely to get close enough to make a good impression.

Downside #2

You know how the Japanese live in close context with paper-thin walls and yet still seem to be unaware of loud activities a few inches out of eyesight? Think of the same cultural barriers operating as bright sunlight bounces off grains of sand from your towel to the beautiful female's towel three feet away. When you come bouncing up and start establishing beach camp, she is going to look through you like you don't exist. Most likely she will either turn over, so she doesn't have to look at your face or get up and move to a less populated portion of the beach.

Downside #3

About that beautiful beach waitress who comes running up carrying nothing but a pad of paper and a smile, I'm sorry to say but she doesn't exist. If by some chance a waitress comes by you'll find that she is a close relation to one of the previously noted sea lions.

Upside: You're not likely to get any tan lines. Bring a lot of 40 power tanning lotion and use it liberally! All over!

Alternative # 5 Make your thingy a media event

Remember Harry Houdini? He used to have himself stripped naked prior to being put into a cell while manacled with a large number of heavy handcuffs. He would be surrounded by reporters who would take pictures and write stories of his confinement prior to his amazing escape. In this day and age, photographs and video come with any significant media coverage. The operative word here is "naked" as in "naked media event." The important thing is that the lack of clothing must seem to be a natural response to the event at hand. Perhaps you plan to be frozen in a block of ice with no obvious natural way to keep warm. (Wait a minute, I think that's been done and it may keep that special part of your anatomy unusually cold.) Better think of something different!

At any rate, come up with your own media extravaganza at which your member can be conveniently invited and exposed to the press. He will get the coverage he covets! It may require you to develop some skills. Perhaps you will need to learn to pick locks! It may require you to learn to survive with primitive tools. (Survive without any modern implements or clothing in the Brazilian Jungle for a week. See what it's like to live with modern-day headhunters!) It's up to you to come up with idea for your special event to keep your lower brain happy and active.

Downside #1

Each media event that you are likely to come up with will tend to bring its own special catch 22 that may impact on the success of your special thingy coming-out party. For example, if you sit on a block of ice for several days (with or without clothing) it is likely to have some impact on your anatomical friend. In the least you are going to experience shrinkage that may invalidate the desire of your member to make friends. At a more extreme level you are likely to freeze it until gangrene sets in. It is important to remember the point here, the media event is less important than the social success of your lower friend. Don't actually do any damage to him!

Downside #2

You may find it difficult to come up with valid media-advantaging situations for your little friend. If you are unable to find an appropriate scenario that fits the bill, don't try to force him where he shouldn't go. If, for example, you aren't really adept at escaping from a grave in which you are buried alive sans clothing, then your thingy isn't going to have a chance to make any permanent friends.

Similarly, if you should happen to actually run into some of those headhunters in the Brazilian jungle, remember they're also likely to be cannibals. And primitive people have primitive rituals. Like eating the heart of the lion to make them brave. And taking or eating the horn of a rhinoceros or thingy of an enemy to keep them virile and manly! You know what I'm talking about here. There are few activities which you can undertake that will be more counterproductive than having your special friend removed just when he is trying to be friendly. Make sure you keep your lower friend alive!

> Upside: If you survive, you're likely to achieve a certain celebrity status with the possibility of fame and riches. If you never make it to the top you can still be on one of those celebrity quiz shows!

Alternative #6 Artfully blend your thingy into a recognized holiday celebration

Now the number of holidays and locales for which this strategy is appropriate is somewhat limited. It may work appropriately in a number of countries on Halloween or in Brazil during Carnival. On the other hand, your successful depiction of the Easter Thingy will probably not be successful.

There are a number of celebrations that will focus on Halloween in any number of major cities. Philadelphia, for example, has at least one or two major Halloween parties every year that are sponsored by organizations which are very flexible regarding the types of costumes and related props that are likely to be seen.

It would be appropriate to observe that a number of costumes that have been worn at these events are composed of nothing more than a layer of paint that has been carefully spread on the skin of some adventuresome exotic dancers. When skillfully done, the result is a work of art in addition to being an effective adornment. Whether at the familiar giant Halloween party or a more local fetish party, there is little to stop an adventuresome male from being made up in a way to depict a Rajah riding an elephant with his trunk swinging manfully back and forth. Perhaps as an alternative, one could carefully create a truthful or prevaricating puppet whose nose tends to grow or shrink while carrying an unusually large pack on his back. I don't plan to come up with all potential costumes here. It is important to leave that to the creativity of the reader. The intent here is merely to provide the concept. My only caveat is to make sure you follow your local ordinances so that no elephants end up in jail!

Downside #1
> The number of applicable holidays is somewhat limited. In most cases the Easter Elephant will end up behind bars. Neither will the Christmas reindeer whose nose grows to point in the appropriate direction be looked upon fondly. Halloween is the holiday here. Make the most of it!

Downside #2
> Cultures tend to differ among organizations and big cities. What might be appropriate in Philadelphia may not play as well in the bible belt. Research your party before attending. Or come with a costume that can be sectionalized as appropriate depending on the situation.

Downside #3
> When parading yourself around in Halloween parties, it is suggested that you don't become too aggressive. Let the onlookers look on rather than stick your trunk directly in the middle of a conservative crowd that might not appreciate the good will and camaraderie of your special friend. Otherwise you may be found in a gutter later.

Upside: If you're lucky, you'll run into one of the body-painted dancers wearing nothing else except her smile. She'll show you the skill with which her costume was put together. Too bad you're wearing the giant prosthetic elephant ass!

Alternative #6 Participate in an erotic art show and include yourself as one of the exhibits

Read those underground papers that depict off-the-wall exhibits and parties. Network with erotic photographers who have displayed their artwork in similar events. When you know the time and the place, show up with yourself on display. Come either as a living piece of art or as the subject of your own carefully prepared photography, in a way that will enable you to strike up conversation with any attendees who might be interested. You can be assured that attendees will have an interest in your display either from an artistic viewpoint or as a pure eroticism. Hopefully you will meet someone who is similarly friendly and attractive to you!

Downside #1
: The big downside here is finding appropriate events to attend. It may take you a while to ferret and hang out with the right underground folks that will be throwing artistic events. Perhaps the art school students will know!

Downside #2
: You are going to have to take the time to determine and create an appropriate exhibit. This may require you to learn the fine points of photography or sculpting and spend time and money to create the right photos or three-dimensional constructions.

Upside: Nobody really cares what you are doing or why you are at an erotic art party. Just go and do your own thing. It's expected that you will be somewhat bohemian. And it's unlikely you will be arrested for exhibiting yourself under those circumstances! Just drink those glasses of wine and socialize amongst the more liberated college professors and Warhol wannabees.

Lest the reader think that it is a necessary to create situations in which his member can participate socially, be forewarned that this is not in fact the case. It is quite common, for example, for a man on his way up to live his entire life without taking overt actions to stimulate the social life of his organ. Perhaps even the large majority of the time the socialization of a male thingy comes as an indirect result of actions taken by the more commonly-in-control cranial brain.

A typical socialization might occur like this. Perhaps you've gone to your favorite bookstore looking for the reading genre you find most satisfying. You're planning to spend a quiet evening in your loft apartment being entertained by your selection comfortably under the covers of your stylish brass bed. As you peruse the book-lined shelves for druidic warrior fantasies written by authors with the first name Terry (because you've noticed that it's hard to pick out a druidic warrior fantasy by anyone named Terry that doesn't live up to its potential,) you find fingers coming in the opposite direction skimming precisely the same genre and precisely the same authors. The only difference is that these fingers are less rough and look more caring than your own! In addition, they are carefully coifed with finger polish that has been applied to smoothly curved nails containing no dirt like your own.

You casually turn your head to the right to see that the hand connects to a not-overly-tanned arm that runs up to a not-overly-tanned shoulder and attaches quite conveniently to the torso of a not-overly-weighty woman who coincidently is not overly-tall or overly-aged relative to yourself. Seeing as how she has passed level one of your first cranial barriers to socialization, you ask if she too is looking for druidic fantasy novels written by authors named Terry.

Momentarily, she smiles at you thinking that you may be a complete boob. Seeing as how you've successfully made contact, you continue to further develop your opportunity by explaining exactly what you are talking about. Fortuitously, she too is looking for novels of the type you just mentioned, however it turns out she was unaware of the druidic-Terry phenomena and you press your advantage. You carefully point out a few other of the Terry collections that will make similarly good reading when she finishes the current epic. (Currently she is on novel three of the six novel set.) During this discussion, conducted while the two of you are both on your knees, you have creatively used that time to put your hands behind your back and dig the dirt out of your most conspicuously dirty fingernails so that you will be more presentable a few minutes later.

(During this short period of time, your cranial brain has made an evaluation of the lady's personality and overall attractiveness. Since she has passed all of your filters and on an intellectual level you feel there might be some sort of connection worth pursuing, you invite her to the bookstore's coffee bar, thinking that you might get to know her a little better and it will show that you are hip.)

"Ya Wanna Go to the Coffee Bar?" you say, and surprisingly she accepts. Although this is a book for a man on the way up we will look into the female mind for a moment. In much the same way that your cranial brain has been processing information, her mind has also been busy. Since she has accepted your invitation to the coffee bar we can draw certain conclusions about her mindset. First of all, she isn't strongly attached to any particular person of the opposite sex. We can tell this because your premise of inviting her to the coffee bar wasn't a particularly strong one. Her acceptance tells us that despite that weak offer, she finds you intriguing enough on some personal level to go find out a little bit more about you. Certainly she has already run you through a number of filters of her own.

On a basic human level she has decided that you aren't particularly dangerous; there is something about you that is at least attractive enough to learn more about; and you may not be the swiftest guy but you obviously aren't spending your complete afternoon playing video games. In this day of hi-tech that may be filter number one! And lucky you, she's ovulating. That has probably obscured some of the rough edges that would normally have blown your cover.

So each of you carry your Terry books to the coffee bar where she orders a Mocha Crème and you, wanting to continue to make a good impression, order that exotic espresso that you've heard about. The coffee vendor sizes you up and asks how thick you would like it, as thick as it should be? You respond "of course" not really knowing much about espresso. After each of you have been served your drinks, you eye the larger cup your companion has been served and compare it to the shot glass-sized mug containing your espresso and suspect that you have been cheated somehow.

After the two of you sit down, she carries the conversation on a number of topics for a while since, after all, you're really a pathetic conversationalist and prefer not to show it! You take a quick swig of your espresso and then realize that it is markedly stronger than the normal coffee you remembered. You choke briefly and then put your glass down while looking enviously at her Mocha Crème. She takes brief pity on you and hands the cup to you asking, "Why don't you try some of mine. You'll probably find it to your liking!"

"She is an angel," you think. Well that may or may not be true but you are certainly moving in the right direction. She has offered you the opportunity to drink out of her cup. This is symbolic of her need to share experiences with someone. In addition it tells you that she has, at least on some level, determined that your germs aren't worrisome enough to scare her off. Thank heavens you were able to clean your fingernails!

When both drinks have been finished, you offer to take her home after purchasing your books. She accepts. This is interesting on two levels. First it demonstrates that neither of you fall into the common category of bookstore swanks who pick up a book, reads it until all of the pages are bent, and then stick it back on the shelf so that nobody else will ever want it. Second, she has accepted your ride home.

After you open the car door for her, (you are extremely gallant today), you squeeze in to sit down with her and notice for the first time, that she is wearing a perfume that smells rather heavenly! Suddenly you get a tingling from your thingy that heretofore hasn't been thinking much at all. You drive into the parking lot of her apartment complex and stop near her door. The car is in park, and you turn to her as she says, "Would you like to come in?" Your thingy really begins to sit up and take notice as you get out of the car and walk, admiring her rather alluring shape from behind as you head toward the apartment to see where she lives.

The door closes behind you and you look at each other. Two sets of lips close the distance as two Terry books go flying through the air, forgotten momentarily. Then your lips begin to move lower; pausing as they caress the now bare breasts of your friend; moving first to one and then to the other; pausing again to probe with your tongue and then gently suck on her nipples and surrounding area. Soon both are wet with moisture, and then your tongue draws a line downward. Her stomach trembles as you work its way casually, then methodically further down. Your fingers slide over the swell of her hips as they slip inside her jeans and panties, slowly pulling them down and removing them to gaze at her well trimmed . . . Well . . . sorry . . . I'm getting a little off track here . . . back to the point of our story . . . .

In the meantime your thingy is thinking its deepest darkest thoughts and longing to be released. And it probably will be, if things keep going in this direction. The point, however, is that your favorite member didn't have to take any overt steps to get this process started. It was your cranial brain that ran with the ball here. And of course your somewhat obscure knowledge of the Terry phenomena.

Now pragmatically, almost everyone has some strange knowledge that they have picked up over time that will, eventually, enable them to connect with the right person. When it does, it's like a key made for the lock. Sometimes it doesn't even matter what kind of knowledge. If two individuals are in the right mood, it will just happen.

So don't go out looking for events that will fraternize your snake unless you think it is so extremely social that ordinary events will not adequately allow it to make friends! You've got a lot of things going for you. It's a statistical reality that even if you do nothing at all other than be reasonably friendly when you meet people, once in a great while something amazing will happen, despite all of the normal odds against it!

CHAPTER 4

Your Part When Drinking!

A number of issues can arise when you consume alcoholic beverages at roughly the same time that you are using your part for its various functions. Most of these issues are not positive in nature for your well-being. Some of them may be obvious and some may not. I will start with the less obvious.

Zipping & Unzipping

I am reminded, in writing this chapter, of my good friend Brendan from many years ago when we attended a major educational institution in the East. It is of course important that I be discreet in discussing what happened to my good friend, so I will do my best to disguise the university so that no one will be able to pinpoint him and comment on his lack of care in maintaining his appendage.

Now many of us back in those days, would regularly attend football games. This was not surprising since it was rare that we would ever lose, thus making for a very positive weekend experience. It became less important, therefore for us to actually watch the game than it would be to party-hearty the night before and during the event. Then when the game was over we could return to the nearest dorms, remove our blue and white clothing and continue to party.

Years later I have realized that our positive winning tradition did not have a positive effect on all concerned. One of my very close friends from our cross-state rival revealed the closely-held secret words of the "Iron City" fight song. That, in fact, their university fight song included the denigrating phrase ". . . . State Sucks!" regardless of who their current opponent was. I think this negative psychological effect was much stronger than the positive effect of our own fight song that essentially repeated over and over again, "We don't know the god-damn words" to the clearly-played melody of our marching band. I know this must be the case because we have not been on each other's schedule for several years, seeing as how we joined the Big 10. And yet they continued to denigrate us. I digress again.

Beer consumption was very popular during these periods and would routinely occur in large quantities. Often, dear readers, it would reach the point that many of us became inebriated and so full of beer that we would have to empty ourselves out before being able to consume any more. This brings me once again to a small divergence from the main thought. If beer is measured in fluid ounces, how is it possible that one beer could be "less filling" than another? It appears on the surface that if you drink 16 ounces of one beer that is described as "less filling" and 16 ounces of another beer, it is likely that the urinal time to make room for each of these beers will likely be the same. I feel confident that if we were to conduct a study on a large population and simply covered the 16 ounce beers with paper bags (so that they couldn't be recognized) and then requested each of our study participants to drink to the point they must relieve themselves (commonly called "breaking the seal") we could, with statistical analysis, prove that 16 ounces of a light beer is just as filling as 16 ounces of a non-light beer.

[The actual study procedure here would not be difficult. We could use the previously mentioned fax method to acquire a large enough statistical sample of beer-drinking participants; break them into two "less filling" and "more filling" groups; carefully allow them to drink themselves to the point that they would "break the seal" while maintaining proper room decorum, and then have one of our study assistants steer each participant with the "urge" into the appropriate peeing booth or convenient restroom. Then the study assistants would carefully direct the participant's thingy into an appropriately labeled jar to ensure no splashage or inappropriate measurements of volume returned. The population (if either) which returned more volume is likely to have found it to be more filling. The more difficult part of this study would be to ensure an adequate number of study assistants was available. This scarcity also could be solved by the fax method.]

[On second thought it would probably be easier and cheaper if we simply put the bags on the heads of the study participants. We could simply cut a mouth hole to stick the neck of the bottle through. Then we could simply have them stand in a line and drink until full. They would raise their hands and that would be a signal for our study assistants. She [or he] would place the participant's thingy in a carefully measured glass and he could relieve himself to the appropriate level without splashage in order to start again. In this manner we would minimize the need to steer drunken participants into a restroom, highly likely to result in stumbling behavior.]

At any rate Brendan was a party hot spot. If he was there, a party must be happening. His energy to drink beer was boundless. If a beer had emptied he would jump up to get another for himself or for you. God Bless Him! And now to the point of my discourse . . .

On one particular evening, on one fine Saturday night, as we were celebrating our afternoon victory, Brendan drank enough beer to forget one of the prime rules of male appendage maintenance. At some point long after breaking the seal, Brendan got out of his seat and energetically rushed to the nearby restroom. After energetically relieving himself in the conveniently available wall facility, he energetically zipped himself up and turned to walk away. It was at that painful moment he realized the zipping procedure had failed and his penis had been caught in the metallic zipper mesh. (For a particularly good re-creation of the look on his face see the movie "Something about Mary.") Brendan had broken an important rule of maintenance which is:

Always put your thingy completely away before zipping up. This is best insured by wearing boxers or briefs to protect your manliness behind a wall of cotton or other fabric. This two-step procedure 1) **put protective cotton wall in-place**; 2) **zip-up**; will go a long way to helping you avoid Brendan's situation.

Fortuitously the health center was right across the street and we threw a long trench coat over Brendan as we hobbled him over to the side door entrance, where one customarily stood in line with other students to see the nurse and be directed for aid. In manly fashion, Brendan stood in line wearing his trench coat behind three or four other students as they were summarily directed to one health practitioner's office or another. Finally he reached the preliminary administrative nurse where we could see the lady mouth the words "What's wrong with you today?"

Apparently his response wasn't loud enough because she had to lean forward to hear it. Or perhaps she just wanted to hear him say it twice! "I've got my penis caught in my zipper."

Keeping the straight face of a professional administrator, she pointed to a room and told him to go sit in the chair next to it. Then she picked up a phone and made a call that rang in the office next to Brendan. Moments later we heard peels of laughter coming from the nurses within. Soon after it died down, a nurse with a serious smile screwed on came outside and directed Brendan toward the door. We didn't see him for another half hour, but when we did, he had an exhausted, much more sober look to him. We then walked him back to his room, where he proceeded to show us his badge of courage. A penis swathed in bandages.

Although this is a chapter on the issues of drinking we want to emphasize the need to be careful in the order of penis replacement to avoid getting stitches on your personal rocket. By always placing your machine behind a wall of cotton or rayon before doing anything else, it is highly unlikely you will injure it by virtue of a drunken upward zipping motion. This is additionally, an important argument to always wear underwear.

Now I know many of us get that unusual life moment when we want to feel free and unburdened by the everyday requirement of layers of clothing, but keep in mind there can be penalties for that freedom. They can be painful. And they can be humiliating! Moreover, sitting on a bar stool and swilling ale for hours can lead to skid marks. And who want to get them on your regular clothing? Not I my friend! Let's move on.

Naked Sports

Uninhibited drinking can also lead to uninhibited clothing-optional sports. Some of these can be more dangerous than others. Chances are, your reflexes will not be nearly as well honed as normal when you play them. This can have bad consequences for your lower appendage.

Naked Baseball/Softball

Remember the jock strap they made you purchase when you took gym class in high school. It was there to protect your overall package from harm, including your serpent. So it is important to keep that in mind the next time you play naked softball and the beautiful girl at bat aims a line drive at your less-than-sober groin.

In addition to protecting yourself from line drives, don't go sliding into first base. The bruises and cuts you get will not be worth it. The fun is in playing the game, not particularly in winning it! If you are the catcher make sure you wear protective equipment. That is one position you don't want to make a mistake in. Don't let the umpire get too close to you either unless that's your style. "Not that there's anything wrong with that!"

Naked Ping Pong

Well it doesn't sound like it should be dangerous. Just remember, in the heat of the battle you will be running away from the table and then running back in. Don't gore yourself on the corner of the table. It's one of those injuries you don't want to have to explain.

Naked Tennis

Well, you must be on your own private court. Lucky you! You have an incredible amount of cash to toss around. Well I can't think of a better way to spend your time than naked tennis with the right partner. Hopefully you can find a partner of the right gender and with the right skill level to keep the game going. If not, just roll around in the net for a while. Make sure you wear your sneakers though!

Naked Hockey
Don't go there.

Naked Twister
Well, it's not really a sport, but if you're going to get naked on a coed basis this seems worthy of sport status. Protective gear is optional, until of course your special friend starts looking for other friends.

Naked Fishing
Now here is a dangerous sport! Imagine yourself out on a boat with three other people wildly whipping lines helter-skelter around your naked body with two or three sharp hooks on each one. If you are a thrill seeker this may be for you. I can't say that the idea appeals to me, however, of having a sharp object embed itself in my privates and then be yanked by a guy drinking his seventh brew. And it will take an hour to get back to the harbor emergency room since you're out on the ocean. Ouch!

Naked Photography
Okay. It's not really a sport either but it's a lot more compatible with having a nice day and you may come away with some spectacular pictures. It's your chance to commune with nature! And make sure you bring some light reflectors and diffusers with you for those sexy shots! Of course if you live in the bible belt, make sure the film developer will develop your shots without calling the local constabulary. Some developers like to censor their services. Ask before you drop your film off!

Bad Judgment

As mentioned in an earlier chapter, alcohol is an enabler that permits your lower brain to wrest control away from its more senior thinking entity. What this means is that your cranial brain is overwhelmed by a partner organ that has completely different judgment parameters. This judgment is usually described as "Bad" by the cranial brain. But often it can do nothing about it.

There are a lot of bad judgment issues that can result from uninhibited drinking. They can easily impact your one-eyed wonder in ways that will make him close his eye and wish he'd done something else. Let's discuss some of the areas of bad judgment that can come back to haunt you!

Waking Up With People You Don't Know

For a man on the way up, it can be something of a downer to wake up in the morning and find that his special friend has been uninhibitedly exploring the intimate regions of someone who fits the description of a double-bagger, or "unattractive individual" as they are sometimes referred. Now this may seem an unkind way to describe someone who may simply have reached that condition through unfortunate circumstances of life. Perhaps she decided to lose several teeth and not have them replaced. Perhaps she began drinking several years before meeting you and never put down the bottle. Or perhaps she just decided to tan in the sun for several years without sun-block and shriveled into something alien. Regardless, you may find yourself in this situation. (On the other side of the coin, some woman may wake up with you sometime and think the same thing, so fair is fair I suppose. But since you're a man on the way up, this is an unlikely situation, of course.) Now admittedly, this has happened to many of us in the past, so no moral superiors need comment. Regardless, *avoidance of double baggers* to whom your thingy may suddenly feel indebted requires continuing vigilance on your part.

A similar type of surprise (but with a certain level of emotional scarring that is likely to result) will occur when you wake up next to another guy. "Not that there's anything wrong with that." Assuming it's not one of your regular companions that you passed out with, waking up with a guy you don't know in a partial or full state of undress will likely cause you to leap right up in the air and say "What the Fuck!" Unless this is your natural state of gender preference, the likelihood is that over the next several months you will be wondering what the hell happened and who was the pitcher and catcher. Hopefully you won't feel any unkind posterior aches that remove all doubt.

First things first however, put on your clothes (watch that zipper); make sure you've still got your wallet and all your credit cards; and run out the door. Let's hope your car is nearby! And I recommend you stop drinking.

The only thing that can make this worse is if you wake up, turn over and find out it was a double-bagger guy. With this revelation you have screwed up on every possible level, even if it was your gender preference! At this point you will need a religious conversion of some sort. Pragmatically you should ignore most of the Christian religions, they don't really want converts with gender issues. And buddy, that's what you have at this point! Perhaps something a little more eastern will help. Lean back and slowly mouth the word OM. That's O-A-H-M (roughly). Rumor has it that it will provide a calming influence on you. And frankly you probably need to catch some serenity!

Don't be so down on yourself. It's not the first time this has happened. How many times have you heard of a guy in a similar situation who woke up; roughed up the not-so-female guy; and landed in jail. Congratulations, you're not in the slammer. That would really add to your concerns because then you would have to explain to someone! Now that you are calm you can logic this through! You were doubtless in some bar in which a large portion of the population was cross-dressed and were too stoned to see straight. Next time you should take notice when your female friend gets a bulge in her skirt. Get yourself a guide when you go out partying!

Trying to Sleep With People you Shouldn't

Back in the 70's, Perry, a mutual friend of myself and Brendan (the zipper guy) made a name for himself by always being able to convince dancers at the local go go bar to sleep with him. It amazed me that he could seem to do this over and over again. I decided to hang out with him and learn his amazing technique. So one day I went with him to the bar and watched the show. Afterwards the extremely attractive dancer came out to meet us and surprisingly she brought a female friend.

I thought to myself, this is my lucky day. We went outside and sat on the local wall and drank beer for an hour before retiring to her apartment room nearby. During that hour it appeared to me that her friend had not been all that communicative, however I presumed that it was the effect of the beer. I hadn't been all that talkative myself having consumed several bottles. It didn't take Perry long to jump in bed with his attractive partner, leaving me and her friend (let's call her Shea) to find a place to sack out. Actually there weren't many other places to sack out other than a lounge chair and the floor next to the bed. At least, there was an extra pillow that they tossed off of the sheets. I put it on the floor near the front of the bed thinking we could stretch out parallel and then who knows? My counterpart with a different plan grabbed the pillow and tossed it on the chair. I thought, "This is a game." So I grabbed it off the chair and threw it back on the floor. Then she picked it back up and threw it on the chair. As I grabbed it from the chair, she took hold of the other end and began to pull. My belief that this was a game continued for a few more moments as we struggled for the pillow. Then something in Shea's expression told me this was not a game. It was a life and death struggle for control of her body and her gender and her soul. (It was an extremely symbolic pillow!) Whereas I was a fairly strong guy, this girl in her twenties was ripping that pillow away with all of her strength and a certain fury reflected in her face that told me she was, yes . . . a lesbian. In that moment of realization I knew that any further socialization between the two of us was completely useless. My friend Perry had picked up a very attractive and bisexual dancer. At that point I lay down on the floor next to the bed and went to sleep. Shea flopped on the chair in exhaustion. Hours later I woke up to the sound of thumping on the bed next to me. I sat up like a wraith in the middle of the night and looked over to see Perry and his friend smiling back at me. That was his secret (or at least one of them). His thingy had amazing staying power and his reputation preceded him.

General Conflicts and Alliances

Your pocket rocket and alcohol exist in a vague continuum of alliance and conflict. Our male perception is that our thingy will be more successful in its eternal search for happiness if the cranial brain allows the body to haze itself with a level of alcohol. Now on one level this may be true, if all of your potential partners have hazed themselves similarly at a party or bar. Alcohol does allow us to let down our barriers. We may become a little more social. Simply holding a bottle or glass in your hand allows you the luxury of becoming a cigarette smoker without the dangers of inhaling the smoke. You can gesture, talk like you're an Italian, and emphasize everything you say. Moreover, by simply drinking a beer or mixed drink and not being obviously attached to anyone at the same location, you can make the statement, "I am available."

Now you might think that this is less important to a guy with a penis (and most of us have them.) That instead, it is the female who needs to make it clear whether or not she is available to spend a little time with you. However this is not exactly the case. It is important to make it clear that you are part of the game. If you stand there stone-cold sober for twenty minutes while talking to a woman holding a martini, one of you is going to begin to feel awkward. The important point is that it will likely be the woman. If you stand there and drink nothing, she is going to conclude that you are planning to leave shortly and are not making any permanent investment in getting to know her. You are killing time. And you are wasting hers also. So whether or not drinking is a negative for your body, in some circumstances it's a requirement if you wish to be social. Thus at an event with alcohol, it is probably to your benefit to drink something. Now if you are a teetotaler at heart, one way around this is to put something else in your hand, like your favorite brand of bottled water. Stick a lime slice inside to make it look official. You may look a little pretentious, however it won't look like you are preparing to cruise to a more interesting location.

So we can see that as a social ice-breaker, drinking may provide some positives to help your favorite fellow. But what are the negatives? After drinking several beers or mixed drinks there can be a number of them!

Toiletry

Bad aim can be a real downer when someone you know is drunk at a party. How many times have you gone into the bathroom at someone's premises and found the seat up and a puddle of piss on the floor! To the doofus from the "can't shoot straight gang," this must seem like a minor inconvenience but for the person cleaning up afterwards it's a drag! It may seem like I'm taking the women's side of this story but I don't want to be wiping up after someone. If I did, I'd go in and spray like a Thompson machine gun myself.

And there's a strong possibility that someone at the party (women most notably) may want to use the sitting position. You don't impress a woman positively when she forgets to look when settling back and ends up half submerged in the bowl along with the urine and floating cigarettes you discarded inside. I think you can safely assume that if there is a higher being who put you here, he was assuming you would use your thingy as an aiming mechanism, among others. Of course as men age, it is somewhat natural in many circumstances that their firing pressure (and consequently aim) decreases. That's fine. But it's still not an excuse to paint the floor.

Who knows, the female mind may assume that if you are unable to hit the bowl from a standing position, it may suggest that your mechanism isn't long enough to get an accurate reading! So for gods sake sit down if you're so short-sighted!

Performance Issues

Stimulation and orgasm are going to become more difficult! Even if your lower brain is able to navigate where it wants you to go, you may not drive over the finish line! So here are some thoughts. If you are a twenty-year old guy known to most women as hair-trigger Hal, you may not have a problem here! (Of course they may not let you into bars in a lot of states). But in this case it may actually be an advantage to have two or three beers before putting your tool to work. That jackhammer may take 15 minutes from start to finish instead of your usual three. Quite an improvement! Now they will call you half-way Hal and you won't have women running away at your approach.

For individuals not facing the hair trigger issue, the situation can be different. You may find that your thingy won't get stiff at all! Imagine that. You worked all that time to meet somebody but you knocked your lower brain unconscious in the process. What a waste! And somewhat embarrassing too! I highly recommend you try to avoid the situation in which you become so stinking drunk that you are dragged away to jail as a nuisance. Alternate a glass of water between every other drink if you must. It will save your liver in the long run.

Okay, you were able to get stiff but you've been working for a while and your partner is doing okay but you're starting to tire.

After another twenty minutes of pumping you're no longer having fun. Your partner has had ten orgasms but even she's getting a little bit bored. What's the problem here? Well it would appear that you've drunk a few brews too many. When you numb your tool to the point that it doesn't enjoy the process, your own pleasure is going to suffer. That orgasm is the release that most of us need to enjoy a sexual encounter. Without it, it's only good for one person. (Except, of course, to the degree that you bathe in the glow of other people's pleasure.) If this problem has never happened to you, take a test! Go home, drink yourself silly, and then do yourself and see how long it takes you. You may not be able to achieve that special moment! Okay, don't do it and just take my word. Why add to your daily frustration level for no reason.

Gymnastic Issues

It's easy to get on the wild side when one has been drinking. You start thinking of that shiny new weight bench that you just bought and the unusual sorts of positions you might try out. Of course you first have to convince your partner. But you can try the one where her feet go up in the air on the bar or the one where she hangs off of the bench doggie style. If you're more adventuresome you might buy one of those leg collar things which you stick your feet into and hang upside down. Who knows! And your imagination may take you anywhere!

The important issue to remember is that you can hurt yourself if you don't take care. The body may look like it can do a lot of things but how many people can actually slip into all of those positions you find in the Kama Sutra? My suspicion is that if variety is important to you, your partner selection may be limited to those individuals who teach yoga in the nearest workout center.

While we're on that topic, for a man on the way up, membership in the local gym with its access to myriad body-shaping classes and cardio heart-honing workouts is actually a good way to meet a lot of nice looking people. Just bop into the one that appeals most to you. It's amazing, for example, how many attractive women are enrolled in the local cardio boxing class. They outnumber the men about 5 to 1. These are women who enjoy staying in shape. And chances are they're also enrolled in that yoga class. These are people your member would like to meet!

But back to the topic at hand. After imbibing a large amount of alcohol it becomes a little dangerous for your member (and in fact your whole body) to jump with your partner on the nearest piece of gym equipment (or recline hanging upside down over the end of the couch.) Gravity can suddenly hurt you, if the full weight of your partner somehow bends your part's hydraulics in ways it was never meant to bend. Worse yet you may just knock the barbell off of its supporting bars and crush something or someone underneath that never should have been there.

Similarly, if you are unusually kinky, suspending people in mid air by ropes and chains could also be quite destructive if the wrong rope breaks or some chain link decides that it no longer needs to be a part of the team. Common sense is an important counterbalance if you plan to live on the wild side. And drinking prior to wild activities will not help you here! Your hydraulics were made to certain engineering specifications just like everything else. You don't want to exceed them for the sake of a moment's pleasurable gratification. The healing period could be longer than you think and will certainly require you to cut down on the type of activities that got you there.

For a man on the way up, there are certain other parameters that are important. For example, it is generally considered to be bad form to be found exercising your special friend in the environment of a corporate office or copy room. Sure, you may want to climb up on that copy machine and hit the button while reaching some level of sexual release, but the look on the cleaning lady when she comes in to remove the trash will be just as priceless as the picture you are making. Such in flagrante activities are not quickly forgotten. Similarly, should you decide to hold a romantic meeting in the board room with another individual from your firm, the probability is high you would be caught. These are the stories of which legends are made. Prepare for them never to be forgotten and to make you stumble on your steps up the corporate ladder. Yet drinking can make a man lose his head and try to perform such activities at precisely the wrong time. There are a large number of senior corporate executives whose careers have been short-circuited through inappropriate on-the-job dalliances. Off-the-job it would simply have been a rumor. On-the-job it becomes inescapable fact.

Putting it where it shouldn't go

Now on some level this may be a matter of opinion, but it is clear that when one has been drinking with motivation, he may decide to use and stick his thingy where he might not ordinarily. Sometimes this will be perfectly okay. If your attractive partner suggests you should stick it in the other place, (you know the one I mean) go right ahead as long as you are completely sure everyone's health is 100%; you are wearing protection; you have a signed and notarized certificate of health from her doctor; you have a lot of lubricant handy; and you are gentle!

Oftentimes this is not the case. You may, for example, find that the certificate of health looks like a forgery. At that point you should be thinking with some trepidation that health hazards are a concern. I'm not going to go into them in detail right now. There is a fairly detailed description of them at the end of the book in the "serious pages." You have, I'm sure, a pretty good idea what they are. The important thing is that you have to constantly be aware of them where your part is concerned and diligently keep it protected from the large number of dangerous gremlins that now float in people's blood; reside in their body fluids; and crawl around in their body hair.

Since use of one's part for pleasure is such an important facet of the male life, I am going to discuss it shortly, but you will have to wait until the next chapter. In the meantime I'm going to continue with the prior train of thought. Let's go back to putting it where the sun don't shine. Most of you will try this at least a few times in your life. Curiosity will make you do it. You'll likely try it after two or three beers. (At least your partner will have had two or three beers.) Just remember that there are limits as to how much of one thing can be placed into another. If it appears that the well-lubricated receiving spot is still going to have a hard time receiving your unusually large male part, I recommend you give it up before you hurt the other party. If on the other hand the fit is good and everyone is having a fun time, go for it. Just remember you're going to need to do some cleanup when you collapse in exhaustion from your wild and kinky sex.

Other places it really shouldn't go

Okay. For those of you who are really lacking in common sense,

I'm going make a short list of other places it shouldn't go under any circumstances.

> Ears
> Nostrils
> Eyes
> Blenders
> Microwaves
> Garbage Disposals
> Vacuum Cleaners
> Wood Chippers
> Vicinity of Chain Saws
> Near Ferocious Animals
> Near Cute and Cuddly Animals that are there for the wrong
>   reason (e.g. gerbils)

Okay. Let's go back to that last point for a moment. I'm not sure if this is myth or not but don't go shoving any small animals up inside of you. This is definitely not being smart with your part. For one thing, something is bound to go wrong and you will end up in the hospital getting some really bad publicity for your part. This is highly likely to send a man on the way up back down again. Let's list some of the things that might go wrong:

- If it's scratching around inside of your body it will likely create cuts that may become serious, requiring hospitalization.
- It might actually bite you from the inside.
- If it dies inside of you it may require removal. It might come out naturally but it might not. Once again, a very embarrassing situation.
- If you decide to go the natural route, you will still be freaking out until it happens.

All of these consequences are bad for a man on the way up. Leave those cute little animals running on their exercise wheels and cedar chips.

Virtual Mistakes

And don't start telling stories about your special part on the corporate e-mail network. I recently received an errant e-mail from a woman who was explaining to one of her girlfriends how she had terminated the relationship of one of her two male lovers. She simply explained to lover A that lover B was the better of the two. (She didn't go into detail here.) She then went on to point out that she told lover A that he had no reason to be going out with her anyhow. She had found out he had recently made another girlfriend pregnant and was dating a third!

My point here is that anything you put down on an e-mail is subject to being misdirected when you hit that send button. If it is salacious enough, it may well set back your career, a poor thing for a man on the way up to do. If you are compelled to send your friends e-mails on the topic, stay away from corporate networks and do it from home.

CHAPTER 5

Shrinkage and Other Complexities

Shrinkage is the quintessential joke portrayed by the character George on the popular Seinfeld television show. George climbs out of the swimming pool, disrobes, and is glimpsed by the woman he is trying to impress. Impression reversal! "Shrinkage" he yells, "it was shrinkage." Speaking as a male, shrinkage is that moment in a man's life when his magic wand seems to disappear, and if in fact size matters to the female of the species, it's a bad time to be seen by the roving huntress. You'd like to be sporting a ten-inch bologna and instead you've got a one-inch thimble that is barely visible. What evil is there in this world that can do more to devastate your image?

If you take a scientific survey of what personal faults men believe would do the most to break their confidence in meeting members of the opposite sex and are given the following choices,

>Bad Breath,
>Toe or Finger Missing,
>Body Odor,
>Low Self-Esteem,
>Balding,
>Tourette's Syndrome,
>Tiny Dick,

invariably the common choice that does the most to break a man's confidence would be a tiny dick. Well, for those who understand what Tourette's syndrome is, there would probably be a few votes for that one. Many women find it more-than-a-little distracting when their date stands up and publicly swears at and humiliates them during that first or second date. And truth be known, this may do more to break up a date than the fact that the same guy has a tiny dick but she doesn't know it yet.

But the fact of the matter is most men are adequately equipped to make a woman have orgasmic pleasure as long as they follow the basic rules and the woman isn't mentally blocked from years of being brought up as a strict Catholic. It appears that many women have been mentally conditioned by over-obsessive nuns during their formative years. Somehow the nuns knew when a stray thought of sex would pass through a poor unfortunate girl's mind, thus resulting in the application of a ruler to the knuckles. I suppose I'm being a little hard on the Catholics here. In truth, mental blockage could be caused by any particularly repressive upbringing. It would be interesting to do a sexual survey on the women of the (uprooted) Taliban culture in Afghanistan. Unfortunately, even in a post-Taliban era, I suspect that the penalty for conducting such a study would include the removal of the part for which this book is being written!

Most men are adequately equipped to give a woman an orgasm! Why do I say this? Because a woman's orgasm is caused by a number of conditions. Not all, however, are necessary to reach the climactic moment. If one is missing another may replace it and open the lock so to speak.

Perhaps we should go over some of the basics here. Since this is a review for many men you may decide to skip a few paragraphs. If not read on and consider the following:

Foreplay

Any experience which is likely to end in orgasmic delight for a woman needs to begin with foreplay. These are the preliminary niceties that enable her to first feel comfortable and secure with her companion. Second, it provides a euphoric feeling that pervades other parts of her body, much as if there is a direct connection between her mouth, her breasts and her vagina (Ok, her thingy.) Third, this feeling enables her to respond to her companion in a way that both become aroused. This arousal is a prerequisite before a woman is likely to have a successful orgasm.

It is important, therefore, to spend an adequate amount of time and effort in foreplay. What the hell, it's fun anyhow. Half of the fun in a sexual experience is seeing and feeling the woman come. (The other half is you coming [for the really uninitiated.]) So make sure it happens and you'll both have a good time.

As a general principle, a dick is not required for foreplay, tiny or otherwise. Predominantly, gentle but firm hands and an adventurous mouth and tongue are the primary tools to be used during this process. It would be fair to say that you should view your female companion as a canvas and your mouth, tongue and fingers as the brushes. There aren't many masterpieces that have been created with a lot of white space on the canvas. So be sure to fill in the spaces liberally.

Let's talk about that for a moment! Where might you go? Where might you not go? Pragmatically, if your playmate has just stepped out of the shower and has used soap all over herself (as we would hope you do when you shower,) your tongue is in a position to go just about anywhere on her body. BAR NONE!

There are a few presumptions that I am making here. First of all, there is a presumption of good health for the woman you are arousing. No one with dread diseases need apply here. I don't care if there is a low probability of HIV/AIDS transmission through saliva. It seems to me if performing oral sex on a woman has even a slight chance of your catching AIDS, then doing it several times is more than a slight chance! And some diseases *are* transmitted in saliva, so if someone has a form of hepatitis or anything else that you might pick up, consult a doctor first or just don't do it! [I focused on the woman in this paragraph because you are planning to arouse her, but if you have a transmittable dread disease, the only appropriate thing to do is put away your dick and hope for a cure.] Or maybe there is one. See the disease details in the serious pages at the end of this book.

Second, I am presuming that the female here doesn't have some relatively minor vaginal health condition or just plain body-odor that for some reason follows her around! I don't know in particular why this would happen but it can. Licking someone dead center between the thighs is very natural to some men on the way up! To others it may be an acquired taste. Both of these modes assume a woman in perfect health, otherwise the result may be both unnatural and in poor taste.

Third, there is an assumption that your friend isn't given to a sudden and uncontrolled urge to fart nor relies on adult diapers. To the degree these presumptions are not true, it becomes fait accompli that you will not be licking anywhere that they prove false!

Now many readers will say, "Hey, Lords, I'm not that kinky anyhow. I would never put my tongue anywhere near where the *sun don't shine!*" My response to you is that there's nothing wrong with your perspective. If you get adequate pleasure out of the menu that you use, there's no automatic reason to add unnecessary entrees. But when you've had the same sexual experience with one person five hundred times you may need to add something new!

But let's get back to foreplay. What parts are important? What parts are sensitive? Well you can go pretty much with the following list:

> Eyelids
> Ears
> Lips*
> Neck
> Breasts and Nipples specifically*
> Stomach—(working slowly down)
> Thighs*
> Toes
> Vagina Exterior and Interior*
> Anus (once again for the more adventuresome)

I've placed a star upon those items that you really don't want to miss. To do so may have you type-cast as less than adept. To include the wider range of items will improve your status. Now I've said that you don't want to miss certain items, but I haven't put them in any context for you. Foreplay doesn't necessarily begin when a person is standing starkers in front of you. It starts when you romantically and gently begin to remove the clothing and can focus on what you find underneath once you've done so. (Practice removing those bras, if they're a problem for you.) Feel free to give a full body massage to your friend once she's revealed herself completely. She will probably respond in kind.

What about bad form, you ask. What are the *don'ts* that go with the *do's*? Well, first of all it is recommended that you do your best to be spanking clean so that she doesn't experience any body odor or cleanliness complaints similar to those that you would like to avoid. Second, don't swish your tongue back and forth while making loud gargling sounds or dig your nose into her navel while you try to nudge her over like a hog feeding in its trough. You might feel this is a good way to introduce her to your rather absurd eccentric side, but more likely she will avoid removing her clothes near you in the future. Third, don't start tickling the side of her abdomen with your tongue or fingers so that she laughs hysterically and never calms down. And finally, don't make a scary sound and jump from behind the couch wearing a hockey mask when she sashays out of the bathroom after primping. These types of sudden and unexpected activities tend to challenge the confidence your friend will have with you. Invariably they will break the mood, which may be difficult to recreate.

Now let's go over this again. So far you've invested a fair amount of time in making sure that your partner is both comfortable and excited by your intimate presence. Why again is it that you've gone to such trouble? It's because by doing so, your companion is going to spend some time in making your own favorite part feel good. So this is clearly an investment in its welfare. Until now, however, you haven't even tried to create an orgasm for your friend, (which will likely come back, in kind, as an orgasm for you). So let's talk about that for a moment. What does it take to create the intense feelings in a woman that create that spark which puts her over the edge? Here's another list:

- Security/Foreplay
- Massaging pressure on the mons pubis
- An insertion of some sort (it could be your favorite member or it could be your two middle fingers) inside your friend's vagina. [Opposable thumbs don't count as fingers here]

- Breast and particularly Nipple licking and sucking.

Let's talk about these items. Hey, isn't this a book about my part you say! Well yes it is, but unless you help out their parts, your own part may not make many friends. So let's go on.

Security/Foreplay
Well we've talked about what it is, but we haven't really put it in context with the female orgasm. The fact is, if a woman doesn't feel secure with you, she is going to have a hard time peaking orgasmically. She needs to be comfortable with you. Generally you will need to start out slow until that comfort level is achieved. If she isn't sure that you're trustworthy, expect to simply wear yourself out. On the other hand, if you want to concentrate on having sex with yourself, you may ignore this requisite activity. If however, like most of us, you would like to have a shared sexual experience, you must include it on your schedule.

Massaging Pressure on the Mons Pubis (The Power Orgasm)
In reaching an orgasm, this may be the single-most under-rated and important technique that can be applied to a woman. It seems to take second fiddle to "finding the g spot" and frankly that spot can be hard to find for a man. As a factor in bringing a woman to an orgasmic peak, all else may pale in comparison. Yet, many woman don't know that they can have an orgasm this way. In a sense this is not surprising. People tend to learn about their bodies by doing things to themselves. In the case of a Power Orgasm, a woman cannot easily do it to herself. (She may be able to find her own g spot though. Her sensory feedback loop is superb.) But let's talk about this for a moment. "Lords, What the hell do you mean by a Power Orgasm?"

Let's imagine for a moment, that you are lying beside your partner on a bed. She is lying on her back. You are lying on your left side with your right hand on top of her pubic mound (the mons pubis). Your middle two fingers might be inside of her, but if so, we would be overlaying another category of orgasmic pleasure, so let's not confuse the issue for a moment. If you slowly begin to massage her pubic mound back and forth (in a head to toe direction), she will begin to experience a certain level of pleasure. If, however, you begin to place pressure, either through arm strength or weight) on her mound as you massage, you will trigger a deeper physical response. As a general principle, she will be unable to do this personally since she can't put any weight on that spot herself. Now, it is important that the hand motion curves down to match her body shape as you push toward the toes. A flat massage would not get the same response. The pressure needs to stay consistently strong to make this work as you curve to her body! "Lords, this is the sort of thing I do all the time. What have I learned here?" Well maybe you do and maybe you don't. But what is clear here is that this action alone is enough to have many women peak without even pulling out your special friend. There are a couple of points.

First of all, it is this pressure that goes a long way to making your female companion have an orgasm when you are using the standard missionary position. It's not so much that your particular tool is especially big or not. That massaging compression of the pubis by your weight will have almost as much orgasmic effect as anything else. (Although you may have to stick a pillow under her to get it to jut out to where your weight can compress it.) Second, in this day and age of dread diseases, using your hands to bring a woman to orgasm may be the safest thing you can do while still sharing a mutual experience. Notice I said safest, not safe. In general, if your hands have no overt cuts, scratches, hangnails, blisters, pimples, festering boils, weeping sores, perhaps I'm getting redundant here . . . if your hands are in perfect shape, the chances of having a dread disease infect you while you're giving a woman a hand job (there I've said it) would seem to be relatively low. Make sure you wash your hands with soap and water immediately and thoroughly thereafter! And if it is important to you to give a woman pleasure, but you happen to be extremely scared of diseases (and rightly so), this may be your best option. You will make her enjoy your company and at the same time she will likely make you enjoy hers!

The power orgasm technique is important and should be used in conjunction with the other bullet points mentioned above. It's important to note that a person doesn't have to be reclined to use this process, although it makes it a hell of a lot easier. If, for example, she was sitting in your lap you could do much the same thing. It would help a lot if you are relatively strong and in good shape because your arm strength is going to have to accomplish what your body weight was able to do much easier.

Insertions

Okay, now we're getting into what is classically assumed to be a requirement for a woman's sexual release. And being honest about it (power orgasm or not) stimulating the inside of a woman's vagina is going to make the peaking process a lot easier. Now you have a couple of options here, some of which will directly impact your own thingy's pleasure and some indirectly.

Having engaged in foreplay for a while, you can simply place your now engorged tool inside of her, build her to a climactic peak a few times and then hopefully do the same for yourself. Alternatively, you can simply skip her part, bring yourself to an orgasm, and earn the label of "Mr. Avoid at all Costs." Regardless of how you wish to be remembered, if you use the direct approach you must be prepared for the possible consequences. Lacking birth control of some sort, pregnancy is a major possibility. Unless you are in a highly monogamous and long-term relationship this is not a smart move.

Sexually transmitted diseases become a greater possibility. HIV/AIDS; various forms of venereal disease (syphilis and herpes, etc.); and by virtue of pubic hair to pubic hair contact even little bugs can jump from one person to the next. (This is not to say that those bugs can't be transmitted without straight sex but the probability goes up.) So there are a number of cons to be considered when contemplating the straight sex approach. Some of the disease-related ones can be cured. Some of them will kill you. That's a rather sobering thought. It's easy to presume that it will never happen to you and yet it happens to millions of people.

Well, I'm not going to go into a lot of detail with the classical sex maneuver. You aren't going to have all that much control over what happens inside of a woman with your tool. Women's bodies tend to differ somewhat and what angle or position feels good to one may not be the right approach for another. (Does anyone really know where the g spot is?) To get that perfect angle, she will need to move your body around a bit or place a pillow underneath her, or shift your weight in just the right manner, or help you control the rhythm of your strokes by pulling you into her. You've got to go with the flow. The important thing is to ask her what feels best so that she knows you want to find that perfect spot or position. Otherwise she may just ride it out (not wanting to hurt your feelings) and never get that climactic moment. Remember you both want to have fun here. *Successful sex is never having to say you're sorry!*

So let's talk about the less direct method for a moment. This doesn't mean that your tool isn't going to get a workout. It just may not happen in the classical fashion. In an indirect approach to a woman's orgasm, you are going to do whatever it takes to bring her to a peak (or several peaks) without using your special member. She will probably not mind that fact that she won't have to worry about getting pregnant and will worry less about catching a disease in this manner. Moreover you won't have to consider the fact that you have a hair trigger and wouldn't naturally last long enough for her to achieve the golden glow using the traditional approach. Or perhaps your member may become numb after pumping at breakneck speed for 30 minutes with no apparent climactic effect for your partner. The numbness you achieve may then preclude you from enjoying the benefits of your mutual meeting. Although a hand job for your friend may seem to be less than you might hope, she is nonetheless going to enjoy it considerably and will happily return the favor. You may have to teach *her* the proper approach for your pocket rocket, however! Before you get started though, make sure your fingernails are trimmed neatly. We don't want any kind of embarrassing accidents because your hand looks like Freddy Krueger's.

In this approach we are going to go back to the reclining position described in the power orgasm, a few paragraphs back. You may find some other position is particularly beneficial, however I'm writing for effectiveness here. You may have a partner that has a particularly difficult time having an orgasm and *we want success!* So my description will take advantage of the power orgasm in describing the quickest method to achieve her desire. My motivation is not to get her portion of the pleasure over as quickly as possible so that you can have yours. I think an appropriate objective for your woman is to have as many orgasms as possible in a reasonable period of time. You want her to achieve a certain level of satiation so that she can then take care of you (maybe once, maybe twice [you animal you]) as a pleasurable returned favor. Intellectually, I think it is important that you have a desire to please your companion. Philosophically, an orgasm emanating from your friend is a physical statement of pleasure that *should* give you substantial gratification as well as her. Enjoy them and provide them as often as you can.

But back to the reclining power position! Inasmuch as you've already engaged in a substantial amount of foreplay, she is ready and hoping that you're up to the task to take her to the party! Assuming she has no physical/health issues that would preclude you from having used your tongue on her vagina she will be quite well lubricated (wet) which will enable you to fairly easily slip your two middle fingers inside of her.

I'm going to back off for a moment and be a little repetitive here. In this day and age you need to know someone (and their background) pretty well before engaging in oral sex. I am unaware that saliva, which does not naturally carry the AIDS virus, can in any way be considered an *adequate* barrier against it. So assuming your preference for a long life, you may not have licked her at all! Let's consider the alternative. Since lubrication is important in the pleasure-process we're describing, you may or may not find it inside of her naturally. Regardless, if you have not done anything remarkably stupid with your hands previously (I mean they're still clean), there is nothing to stop you placing your fingers inside of her mouth in a somewhat lustful/sexual fashion and lubricating your finger tips with *her* own natural saliva. The chance of catching a disease has just decreased significantly. Now you can slide your fingers inside of her a little more adeptly! Let me point out that most women will get quite lubricated simply from your licking and sucking their nipples. If not, then you can steal some saliva from her mouth as discussed above.

Once inside, your fingers may curl a little bit for the most stimulating position (and this can vary based on a woman's body shape) but pragmatically, the most important aspect will be the level of massaging pressure that you apply to her pubis with your palm, starting slower but then speeding up to increase the intensity.

Remember, your palm massage should follow the contour of her pubis with pressure. This will naturally slip your fingers in a little deeper on the down stroke. It's a little like revving up a motorcycle throttle. (Just a tiny bit, your fingers aren't really going in and out in the power orgasm. It's a massage technique!) Keep in mind that your body weight is replacing that natural weight that would occur in the typical missionary position, although it is concentrated on one (very good) spot.

Breasts and Nipples!

To achieve that orgasm requires a combination of events. First is foreplay, which gets everyone in the right mood with the correct euphoric and lustful feeling. (This will usually include play with the breast and nipples as a part of that process.) Then typically there will be some form of insertion, either in a traditional sexual fashion (if you know the person well and have some form of pregnancy protection) or perhaps with a power orgasm induced hand job. In many situations this will not quite be enough to have her get that last required stimulation that causes her to peak for you. It is common that to achieve that slightly higher state, you will need to continue concentrating on whichever of the two forms of vaginal stimulation you are using, and then at the same time, return to her nipples/breasts with your mouth. That extra combination will oftentimes put her over the edge. You may always need to do this to get her over the top! From an efficiency viewpoint it will increase the number of orgasms she receives in that reasonable time period we've already discussed. Which is a positive! And what the hell, it's fun anyways. It's not like you want to get paid before you do this!

I'm not quite sure how we got off on this track but by now you should be able to make your woman fly high, which is important for a man on the way up. Your tool should be quite happy, whichever method (direct or indirect) you choose. However on the indirect side there may be some direction required on your part if your lady is not particularly experienced in such matters. If she has not provided any male hand jobs in the past it is likely that the first one will not go smoothly. So it will be up to you to tell her what is important. So expect to offer some rather frank advice.

The Obvious Points

Even a completely inexperienced woman will know one or two things. She will know that she is about to grope and find something that hangs like a thick finger and is expected to grow into something bigger. But that knowledge is not enough to make a male have an orgasm. Here's how the typical first brush with a penis will go for a woman this inexperienced (that is, she is trying out her first hand job.)

Initially she will be a little taken aback by the nature of the thing. The throbbing nature gives it a certain life (it has a brain you know) that will cause a certain wonder. Quickly this will give way to the second piece of information that she knows, that it is necessary for her to stroke it. She may, of course, try out oral sex just to see what it's like. But more likely she will begin to stroke it up and down waiting to see if it explodes or does something different. After about three minutes of this you may be in agony since no one has explained yet that you need to have it lubricated. Shortly thereafter you will have to either stop her, or let your tool slowly turn red and wilt from the sandpaper effect! This type of a beginning will not give her confidence and her embarrassment may cause her to give up on you and find another potential boyfriend for a new start. So if you like her, it is important to explain certain facts.

Point #1

Although your tool may provide the initial lubrication, it will soon be used up and require more. This may not be true for an eighteen-year old guy with a hair trigger, but for many of us this will be the case. Now for those guys with an innate sense of being prepared, it is possible that you may be carrying a small bottle of skin care lotion which you can whip out and hand to your friend. If she is not taken aback by your implementation of the "just-in-time" inventory system, then she will smile, tell you what a quick thinker you are, and douse your rocket in a mound of white. Soon you will be highly lubricated, in fact if you are wearing pants you likely have a big wet spot in your crotch. Ah! But it will be worth it!

Many women will, to the contrary, be put off by the fact that you have a squeeze bottle of hand lotion with you and decide that the whole situation is just a little too contrived. Having the bottle of hand lotion will be a little bit over the top.

On a more down-to-earth level, after you explain the need for lubrication, you will have to make note of the fact that her saliva will do just fine! Let's hope that saliva does not carry many diseases! Hopefully she will not be grossed out by this requirement! [Well it does carry hepatitis B! Let's assume for the moment you've been vaccinated.]

So point #1 is: Quickly explain the need for your tool's lubrication if she appears to be unaware of it. As an aside, if she really does go for the skin care lotion, you'd better carry a bottle with you at all times or never expect any sexual spontaneity!

Point #2

Given that this may be her first encounter with the male organ, her stroking motion is likely to be more of a grappling/groping motion that does not effectively stimulate your miniature alter-ego. Sure it feels good, but after a while you start to get frustrated because her technique hasn't developed yet.

It is highly likely that you are going to have to give her a technique to work with! Now I hesitate to define for you what works best. Frankly your favorite motion may not be mine. Regardless, you may have to give her a lesson and explain that her motion up and down the shaft shouldn't require her to grip you like a 20 lb dumbbell and that a stroke that extends over the head of your penis may (or may not) be the kicker that makes your orgasm happen. It is up to you to help her achieve your own golden gratification. The mere fact that she is trying indicates that she wants you to go there!

So point #2 is help her help you come!

Point #3

It is not unusual for a woman having her first experience with a male orgasm to stop the process as soon as it starts. She works you up until you start to climax and when the first spurt flies through the air, she is struck by the sight, (or is literally struck) and immediately quits making the motion that brought you there in the first place, about twenty seconds too soon. You are so distraught that you grab yourself and start pumping to finish the job!

Well, hopefully you won't do that or she'll either expect you to do it all of the time or be embarrassed, once again, by her lack of experience.

This is one of those situations that you pretty much have to play in real time. Although you could try and explain it ahead of time, it's not something you are likely to do or succeed at explaining, (once again it seems a little too contrived or well planned.) So I think what you are going to have to do here is fall back on the overused phrase that crops up again and again in the annals of sexual jokes. Which is of course, "don't stop." Or alternatively you could grab her hand, keep it wrapped around your tool and say "keep going," to avoid the over-used cliché.

So point #3 is help her help you keep coming! Our objective here is maximum orgasmic pleasure and not just for her! So make sure it works out for both of you.

Since we've gotten so detailed here I think I may add a few more thoughts. Not everyone has the same kind of orgasm. Some may be quiet; some may be accompanied by screaming; some may be followed by intense muscle spasms, etc. So if you're the kind of guy whose eyeteeth grow longer and hair grows out of your ears during the process, just let your companion know that they will fade back into your head as the orgasm subsides and you really aren't dangerous. In fact you will simply be having a great time!

It has occurred to me now that this is the chapter on shrinkage. So what causes shrinkage you ask? Well it seems to be caused by two basic reasons. First of all, it is protection against unwary elements that might lower the comfort level of your thingy and (more importantly) his two dangling friends that carry your future generations. Cold temperatures that you find in a swimming pool seem to get the label of shrinker #1. George, or at least the publicity that goes with that particular show has advertised it over and over again. Shrinker #2 is the intense concentration of activity that occurs because of stress or during athletic events. If for example, you are taking a casual walk in the jungle and a tiger steps into the clearing, the stress (a fight or flight reaction) will send all blood in your body into the extremities that will be likely to save your life. Your thingy will not be helpful here. Similarly, if you play racquetball for an hour or two, your body is going to send your blood supply almost anywhere else in your body except for your penis! It will get the short shrift! (Ok I guess the pun was intended.) So the next time someone spots you with shrinkage you can turn to them and say, "Well I guess that proves I'm the most athletic guy among us!"

That won't work you say? Then I guess the best thing to do is not to be spotted with shrinkage. Of course this is pretty much out of your hands and in Murphy's. The bottom line, per Murphy's Law, is that if you are in a condition of shrinkage, at some point your bathing suit will slip down or if you are running on the tennis court you will dive for a shot, fall down, and your tennis clothes will be scraped off you by the asphalt. Poor you. Both shrinkage and a trip to the doctor to get it fixed in one unfortunate accident!

On to other topics. "So Lords," you say, "should I dress left or should I dress right?" For the less-than-initiated, this is a question that relates to whether you should let your penis hang down the left side of your pants or the right. First of all this is only a question if you are one of the guys that wears boxer shorts. If you are wearing briefs, then this question will never come up because your penis will find its own perfect way to lie down thank you very much. Now for those boxer wearers who feel the need for a more complete answer here I'm going to point out the first level response which is: *nobody cares*! Next, however, I'm going to back off slightly and say that somebody cares. It's the tailor of your $2000 custom made suits. He may, in fact, ask you whether you dress left or right as he stick his hands down the front of your pants to see how close the inseam is coming to your crotch. If, god forbid, it turns out that you are not wearing any underwear he will be doing his damndest not to run into your special friend. And any preliminary intelligence that you are willing to give him on this topic will be of some aid.

Now a related issue that tends to ride with the boxer-wearing crowd is that it is important to know whether left or right in order to more properly position that 10 or 15 inch monster that you are sporting. The implication here is that your bad boy is so big, the only way it will fit in briefs is if you roll it up like a hose of Italian sweet sausage. Since that apparently is not a good answer, you must therefore choose an appropriate leg down which it will dangle. Now the obvious answer to the question is, "Pick the most comfortable leg." If, however, you are looking for a more sophisticated answer, then I will have to fall back on logic.

The answer to your question will depend on your fashion sense. In particular, it will relate to which leg you tend to apply wrap-around handkerchiefs or bandannas for that Jimi Hendrix look. Clearly if you are going to tie tourniquet-like objects on either of your upper thighs, then you will wish to dress down the other leg. So a Rambo-like fellow who expects to be shot several times in his leg should do his best to predict where those bullets will strike and dress to the other leg. Actually this is for two reasons. He will want to avoid placing his penis where he is going to have to tie a tourniquet and in a related logic, he will prefer to place his penis where it is least likely to be shot off.

Similarly, if you are one of those people who regularly reads the duct-tape book and are likely to use it to wrap around one of your legs as a patch for your jeans with holes, then I would recommend choosing the other leg to dress down. Otherwise you may find your thingy stuck to the tape at an inappropriate moment.

CHAPTER 6

Everyday Commuting

Most of us spend about two hours a day (one hour each way) commuting in and out of our everyday jobs. Some of us drive our own personal cars. Many of us spend this time on public transportation such as a regional rail train or bus. We jump on that train at 6:30 in the morning and arrive near our work location around 7:30 a.m. Then we leave at 5:00 in the evening and get home an hour or so later. In the meantime, most men on the way up will spend the day working. But at the same time they will be splitting their concentration. The majority of their thoughts will be on the work at hand, but occasionally sexual thoughts will stray into that work-a-day mix. Perhaps you'll start thinking about that beautiful secretary sitting down the hall. She was wearing a lovely short dress today! If you're driving a cab, perhaps it's that beautiful dispatcher at the home location or the attractive fare you just let off. These types of thoughts pervade our lives and can occur at any time of the day. They are often strongest when we have idle time, such as when riding on that regional train during the commute home.

Now when a man on the way up rides a train, there are several things that he can do. He can take work home with him and dutifully work on it during the ride. He can elect to catch up on his sleep if he has a snooze alarm to wake him up before his stop. Or, being the astute networker, he may elect to be sociable with other people on the train. Now a young man on the way up tends to make friends easily. And it is likely that he will make as many female friends on the train as males. In fact some men tend to use the train as a means of finding friends, (since they are so tied up in their everyday occupations.)

Each train has five or six cars and, if desired, he could (roughly) walk through 100 people per car until he found some attractive person to sit down with and strike up a conversation. In addition, if this were a really important activity and he had some office flex-time, he might take a train that leaves the station at 7:30 and arrives a little later than most. Generally this enables one to ride with a higher percentage of secretaries and the opportunity to meet attractive companions would be greater. Of course, as a man on the way up, one must follow the dictates of his work culture, which may require an earlier morning appearance. But who knows, perhaps he would have that flexibility!

Now first, let me point out that there are categorical differences in the types of males who move around and elect to sit with women in the sociably-designed two or three-rider seats typical of such a train. The first kind sits down, brings up a topic of conversation when the opportunity arrives [he may look at the book she is reading and make a connection], and then spends some time learning about the lady he has slyly elected to meet. Sometimes he decides he has learned enough and opts to sit in a different location the next day. Occasionally he finds himself quite attracted by the woman at hand and sets up an opportunity to meet her later.

The second type of fellow will also walk through cars and look for women to sit with. After seating himself next to the unwary lady, he never actually socializes. Instead he will pretend to read his book while occasionally stealing glances at her presumably lovely legs while imagining he might have some sort of relationship with her. This second fellow is not actually considered to be a "man on the way up." Instead, after his modus operandi has been repeated a number of times, the women on the train will catch on and consider him to be a "lurker." As casual as a man might appear as he moves up and down the train over a series of months, stealing glances at beautiful legs, ultimately he is going to be noticed by the female crowd. Soon they will have appended a descriptive name to him based on some facial attribute or physical feature. A collective buzz will disseminate though the population from the more vocal females about "crab-nose" or "fish eyes" as someone to avoid. Now I believe that a man has to go out of his way to deserve and acquire the "lurker" label. But having talked about this with a number of women who have spotted them, the prime identifying characteristic is not hard to see. The typical "crab nose" will get on a train that still has 40% of its rows empty, yet will (after gazing up and down the car) still manage to sit down next to a woman, making her feel crowded. Let's face it. Barring some other motivation, most people tend to look for an empty row of seats on the train. We (at least in the USA) generally like our personal space. So unless you wish to be branded a fish-related name (which seems to be the genre), make sure you have some actual social motivation in your intrusion rather than simply the desire to ogle. The principle here is that oglers bring nothing to the table except a lot of not-so-stealthy glances.

There's an old cliché that all women are extroverts and all men are voyeurs. The first part of that cliché comes with certain parameters around it. All women may be extroverts, (but only for people they prefer to have looking.) For the second part, no parameters are necessary and women know it. So unless you're a twenty-two year old handsome dude with muscles, you'd better start up a conversation before glancing excessively!

Now a young guy on the train will, over time, develop certain levels of friendship and candor with the females on the train (unless he prefers the other gender.) He will find some women who are purely conversational in character, that is, they like to talk on the train but never take the time to meet after-hours; he will find some women who would like to meet for drinks before heading home on a Friday night; and he will find some women who are more flirtatious, to the point that the sexuality of their conversations is hard to ignore.

And now comes the reason for the chapter. If a man on the way up flirts his way to a certain point among this last group of friends, he will ultimately meet someone who has a similar adventuresome flair. This person will not back down from the dare tactics that occur when someone asks more and more intimate questions. Now these may not be the type of questions you ask when you first meet someone. Over time, however, as people develop relationships, they tend to ask and be asked more and more direct questions relating to intimate thoughts. You may, for instance, rather pointedly reach the question, (and it's somewhat logical in this situation) "So, have you ever thought about having a sexual experience on the train?"

Of course at this time it is no longer your cranial brain talking. I would like to point out that it is quite common to have this kind of a conversation amongst a group of men and women who know each other well on a Friday beer night out. Usually these kind of questions fall into the genre of "So, have you ever done it with another woman?" Or perhaps "So, do you swallow?" However, the difference here is that the large group of people has become inured to provocative questions over time and enjoys either the directness or the trust that the group conveys. This intimacy sparring is often driven by the cranial brain just for fun.

On public transportation in a row of side-by-side seats, it may well be the southern brain that is doing the thinking. And when you have finally met the right adventuresome companion, your part may start getting smarter all of a sudden. Knowing clearly that your friend is daring you to do more, you must recognize that you are riding on public transportation with people sitting all around you. Then it is up to you to surmount the obstacles. It is also necessary to recognize your limitations.

The Generic Approach to Your Partner's Arousal

Let me re-emphasize that this approach presumes that your partner is willingly complicit in this process. First, it is important to borrow one of the fundamental magician concepts in working a miracle, which is that you must hide what cannot be seen. Let me describe a hypothetical as to how and what, can and will occur.

You've discussed the topic of sexual experiences on the train and you look her in those beautiful eyes and say "So what would you think about having one?" If her follow up is "We may have to try it sometime!" then you've effectively been green-lighted to try it now! I'm going to make a few assumptions here. Assumption #1 is that you have a briefcase of some sort, although it could be a hefty student backpack or something of similar size. Assumption #2 is that you have a full or even half-size newspaper with you in that briefcase or pack.

If your briefcase is on the overhead rack, you must of course remove it and place it on your lap. Then pull out the newspaper and open it up on your briefcase so that it covers the lap of both you and your friend to a substantial degree. Your hand that is between you and your friend must then go under the paper, allowing it to roam freely on her thighs. The briefcase will provide a little vertical distance between your friend's lap and the paper covering it. As a result, you will be able to accomplish certain things without any noticeable paper movement being visible to surrounding passengers. It should be easy for you to massage your partner's outer and inner thigh with relative abandon. The level of excitement for both of you will be somewhat dictated by her clothing. If she is wearing a pants suit, it may be somewhat limited, given that your massage will be though a layer of clothing. If on the other hand she is wearing a relatively short skirt you will be able to slip your hand below and pull it up underneath the paper. If you are lucky, she may additionally not be wearing any pantyhose, thus increasing the arousal for both of you substantially. And if you find that she is wearing neither pantyhose nor underwear then you are not lucky at all. In fact, she likes you and has been anticipating this (or a similar) event.

At a point you will recognize certain limitations. First are the surroundings. The conductor will walk past occasionally looking for tickets and staring into your lap. His approach may be intimidating and your position will look slightly suspicious. It may become necessary for you to place the hidden hand back on top of the paper for that inconvenient moment of ticket review, or perhaps when a line of people is exiting the train and staring down at your seats. You want your companion to enjoy the experience, not be intimidated by it! This particular issue can be partially avoided, however, by making sure the tickets are in such plain view that the conductor doesn't have to look for them.

A second issue is the type of motion that can occur. Obviously your paper can't be jumping up and down like there is some sort of animal underneath. No one will believe your explanation that there is a small gerbil in your lap.

The third and most limiting issue is the structure of your wrist bones. You will find that your wrist structure does not mind providing leg massages to adjacent passengers. It will however, rebel should you try to insert your fingers inside of your friend. You will find that your wrist is not as flexible as you would have thought under the circumstance and that your wrist is getting a cramp from trying to do what it was not designed to do. If, however, she is enjoying the thrill, you may be able to go further.

Enhancing Your Partner's Arousal

In order to achieve a position which may enable you to play further with your friend, you must ask her to slip down in her seat so that your elbow can extend and no longer be crushed against your body, thus enabling your wrist to assume a more natural position in its search for hallowed ground. Frankly, unless she slips into this position or you move uncomfortably away (from a stealth viewpoint) your wrist will attempt all sorts of unsuccessful contortions that you will find to be quite awkward.

An additional advantage of having her slide forward in her seat is that she will be able to make herself available from the waist (with your hand slipping downward beneath the waistband) if she is able to loosen her belt and zipper unbeknownst to the other passengers. Remember, we've got that stealthy paper to cover some of these movements. In this manner, a wider range of clothes (e.g., jeans, etc.) can be worn while successfully reaching a higher level of stimulation.

Alternative Methods of Engaging Your Companion

Assuming you have known your friend for a while and would prefer to have a more reliable method of public transport sexual experiences, you could as an alternative take your friend's trench coat, which will naturally act as a cover, and cut a hole in the interior of the side pockets. By doing so you would be able to stick your hand through the pocket and extend it into the interior of her coat relatively unseen by anyone else. You might, however, still elect to use a paper to camouflage the arm entering her coat pocket. It's a good idea to avoid an embarrassing revelation to the other passengers or they will begin watching you on a regular basis for entertainment value! Obviously, this alternate methodology assumes that you are not simply enjoying a one-time event resulting from your social prowess. It presumes instead that you and your friend are routinely kinky! More power to you.

For both the generic and alternative methods described, you will still have difficulty bringing your friend to orgasm. The amount of effort needed will usually exceed that which can be hidden by our innocent newspaper. Your best bet to achieve such a level will only occur if your friend is very susceptible to orgasm from your inserted fingers at a specific spot inside her (e.g.., her g-spot, etc.) From this side position you will not be able to create the pressure required for a power orgasm. Generally it will be difficult to hide a true orgasm under these conditions, so a medium-high level of stimulation without completion may be your best bet anyway. It always creates a stir on the train when moans of pleasure cascade from the seat in front!

"But Lords," you say, "I don't ride the train, I ride the bus!" Well, that is a problem! In general, buses (at least city buses, the ones with the plastic seats) are not conducive to sexual experiences unless the passengers around you are fall-off-the-cabbage stupid. You may have to rent a room.

This same arousal processes described above can be used on airplanes, however. Simply lift the seat armrest into the upright position so that your hand can wander appropriately. You additionally have the opportunity to take advantage of one of the airline-provided blankets to better hide your passionate play. Just remember that seats on a plane are filled with passengers that have nothing to do and nowhere to go for an hour or two. As a result they are looking for anything to break the boredom and you may provide the windfall entertainment they are looking for!

Now the thought may occur to you that the discussion of the last page or two is focused on making your female partner "get off" as much as you can. It doesn't directly give your tool specific pleasure. Keep in mind that she will ultimately want to return the favor! You may not get the chance on the bus but your apartment is starting to look pretty good right now!

The Mile High Club

You haven't really joined the mile high club by engaging in the process described above while on an airplane. It is an axiom of being a member, that you had the gall to go into the airplane restroom with a companion and wildly coupled in some fashion. It's in the charter rules that while doing this, you may well have caused other individuals to wait impatiently in the aisle with their feet tapping.

To join this club you have to have a lot of chutzpah and be willing to drop your drawers in a tiny cramped space that will get even tinier with a second person. My only advice here is the missionary position does not apply.

Well, I've got one more piece of advice. Apply a little subtlety here. Don't go tripping down the aisle to the back of the plane holding hands. Instead, the first person should go and occupy the room (which the second person should visually see and identify in order to avoid the embarrassment of knocking on the wrong door!) Approximately 15 seconds later your companion should follow. If you see that she is on schedule, feel free to leave the door unlocked so she doesn't have to knock. If not, you may have to keep the door latched to avoid having an unexpected friend join your love nest. Keep in mind that you will need to join the club quickly. If not you will find a small but interested crowd when you re-embark into the regular cabin!

Trains Planes and Automobiles

There are few people who haven't tried to make it in the backseat of a car at some time. It's a natural flow in the evolution of independence from your parents. The negatives here are fairly self-evident. You won't get a lot of headroom (unless perhaps you're in a Hummer). You will need to find a relatively secluded spot (well that's part of the romance). Regardless, you will certainly have a good time. Keep in mind that Murphy's Law dictates that at least once in this type of situation you will be observed by a passing police car and they will stop to tap on your window with flashlights. Be prepared to show identification and be temporarily separated (they want to make sure you are not holding a knife on her.) It will be embarrassing but you will get over it. The amusing thing here is that if you are older (i.e., in your 30's or 40's) they may charge you with public indecency. Hopefully you will see them coming and clothe yourself before they look in. In your teens or 20's they will probably let you go with a warning. This is the natural evolution of beauty and aging at work. When you're in your twenties and on the way up, you're attractive enough to get naked. Having reached your 40's and 50's, people wish to see less of you! The moral here is to get a lot of exercise and keep that gut flat! By the way, if you think the back seat of an auto in a train station parking lot is a natural transition from your previous train activities, it may make sense to think again. The police regularly patrol such lots to protect the cars of people parking during the workday.

The Front Seat of the Car

Many of us have at times decided to enjoy each other in the front seat while actually driving somewhere. This can be a one-directional operation (in either direction) or even a bi-directional process. If you are the driver and your companion is the recipient of the pleasure, she will probably have to slip down in the seat as described before in order to enable you to insert your fingers where they will provide the most pleasure. It may be possible to provide an orgasm in this manner given that she will have the flexibility to move into the most beneficial position. Nonetheless it will still require a substantial amount of arm strength to reach that peak. The unfortunate thing is that you will not be able to deliver your full concentration on your companion, since it is imperative that you continue to drive between the yellow lines, being sure to come to a stop when the vehicle in front requires it. Given the difficult leverage involved in this angle and the splitting of concentration necessary, at a point you will likely tire from the effort. Assuming you haven't reached your destination, oftentimes *you* will then become the direct recipient of pleasure.

If you are driving during the night, you may be lucky enough to avoid potential problems from passing truckers who pull up beside you in a cab four feet above your seat and enabling a direct line-of-sight. If driving during the day, however, it will do you some good to exercise a little discretion. Once one trucker sees you, he will be inclined to radio a number of his friends who will be waiting for you to pass with anticipation. Soon you will be leading a convoy of friends that you never knew you had.

The good thing is that as a male, you are going to have pleasurable options that you never really had on the train (unless it was completely deserted.) On public transportation any motion that would have been capable of creating your climactic moment would have been capable of drawing a climactic crowd. Your newspaper would have been bouncing up and down as if a kangaroo rat lived underneath. The ladies sitting nearby would have been keeping time as if a metronome was ticking back and forth. In a car, however, you need no longer camouflage everything. Your beautiful companion will be able to please you, if she so chooses, in a number of ways. This is when your favorite tool gets to shine in the spotlight.

As a general principle, you will not experience a high probability of catching a dread disease here, since there will be no direct thingy to thingy contact involved (unless you are maniacal [and stupid] enough to put two people in the driver's seat.) Instead your friend will either give you oral pleasure (which you can never really complain about in any event) or a manual polishing with her hand. [See the Serious Pages at the end of the book to see what you could catch.]

But can you sit back and simply enjoy the action? Well, to some degree, but safety becomes a high priority in this situation. The whole activity will become quite dangerous. Now I admit that many of us will risk this danger, but the distraction to your driving skills is immense. Consider the risk you will take as your eyes start to turn backwards in your head at the climactic moment. You'll be driving in reverse! And I am always reminded of the unfortunate accident that occurred in the book "The World According to Garp." Should a crash occur during an act of oral sex you will need to be lucky to ensure that your friend's teeth don't actually remove your favorite part as collateral damage! Rather than experience this unfortunate change in lifestyle status, I recommend that you minimize the number of sexual experiences while guiding multiple-thousand-pound vehicles. The result may not be worth it. And by the way, I guess you can complain about *one* thing related to oral sex. You may find a companion who believes that it is sexy to scrape her teeth along your manhood. As some point you will have to either admonish her or prepare to let your Taliwacker recover for several days from the irritation it has received. My advice is to tell her that teeth and male organs do not mix and should be kept separate.

Motorcycles

Although the imagery associated with motorcycles is a very sexual one, as a practical matter it is effectively impossible to have one person provide another with a sexual experience while seated on a traveling motorcycle. Even if your companion behind was somehow able to reach between your legs and unzip you (a difficult position indeed,) your concentration on the road and inability to receive enough pumping action would negate the benefits. The activities involved in doing so would additionally make an already dangerous vehicle much more dangerous! (Many of my friends broke their legs on motorcycles.)

One possible exception! You may find that your female friends will, with very little help on your part, get somewhat of a sexual experience simply by sitting on the back of that powerful vibrator. Many women have said they enjoy the experience of sitting on a throaty Harley and feeling the power that is emoted!

CHAPTER 7

Your Part in Exotic Locations

It is an axiom that a man on the way up will ultimately walk into a topless bar. In fact most men, whether on the way up or not will make their way into one of these exotic locations a number of times in their lives. This will present a number of conflicts between your upper and lower brain. In addition, it is an unusual situation in that female part(s) will be actively socializing with your own male one (usually by simply waving at you), except that it will be an artificial socialization. The female parts will be soliciting cash instead of just getting to know you! To the degree that women experience the dichotomy of an upper and lower brain, for women in *these* places, the upper brain is usually in control. Although it might appear that anything goes, usually it doesn't!

Let's take, for a moment, the types of bars you might walk into. They come in many sizes, shapes and attitudes:

>Non-Urban Exotic bars
>Urban Exotic bars
>Gentlemen's Clubs
>BYOB All Nude bars
>Triple X establishments

These locations all tend to operate with different characteristics and sometimes varying by time of day. A man on the way up will need to differentiate between these bars in order to distinguish himself amongst his golfing peers and other acquaintances. It wouldn't, for example, make sense to tell everyone to meet at a BYOB bar after the golf match and find that nobody knew to bring three or four six-packs of their favorite brewery products. Let me guide you, therefore, through the various sights and sounds you might expect to experience at each of these different bar locations.

The number and variety of these bars varies by region. You might, for instance, not expect to see as many bars operating in the bible belt, as you would living in the heart of Texas, which appears to glory in the number and variety of unclothed women available for your inspection. Just look in the local phone book! Even in the heart of the bible belt you will likely find exotic bars in urban locations. After all, where there are a lot of men, you will find a lot of bars and a lot of women to populate them. And for many women, this is excellent way to make cash with a minimum of training. There's no need to go to a four-year college to make a man shell cash out of his pocket. In fact, should you line up and query several dancers, you are almost guaranteed to find that at least one of them is currently paying her college tuition (for a subsequent career) by encouraging you to stuff dollar bills in her minimally designed garments.

For women who are particularly attractive and are able to work in the upscale bars, the cash proceeds can exceed six figures annually. And the federal tax rate on dancer income is unusually low. Thus dancer dollars go far in a struggling economy.

Non-Urban Exotic bars

Non-urban exotic bars are scattered throughout the heart of America. They reflect capitalism operating as Adam Smith always anticipated, that there would be an invisible hand slipping dollars wherever those dollars satisfied the greatest need. You won't find many establishments like these in Saudi Arabia or Iran, but you needn't look far in the USA. You can find them anywhere, but they tend to operate in the fringes between developed areas, since no self-respecting township council wants them nearby. Regular customers tend to populate these bars, and operationally they may simply be beer drinking establishments with ancillary entertainment. In this bar genre, there are commonly two or three dancers, each of whom gets up on stage to writhe around a pole (no respectable topless bar lacks one) for her three songs before walking around the bar to collect her tips from the patrons. During her medley under the stage lights, she will dance with varying degrees of clothing on. Song number one is normally performed in fully clothed mode (fully clothed for an exotic dancer). In song number two she will more often than not remove her top to reveal a well-rounded pair of bosoms, which most men find to have a strangely attractive and hypnotic appeal. If you doubt this, simply line up a few topless women beside a road and make observations of men in the cars that ride past. Invariably their heads will turn and mouths will drop open as they whiz along their merry way.

One theory to explain this is that breasts look a lot like those hypno-coins we used to see years ago widely advertised in the back of comic books and guaranteed to hypnotize any subject. You could rotate them and get an optical illusion that would catch your attention and draw it to the center like nipples. According to this [the hypnotic] theory, breasts are simply flashy attention getters! My own belief is that we simply like them, based on a millennia of evolution and being comforted by them. I can additionally say with certainty that although I did read comic books, I have never had the urge to lick or suck on a hypno-coin.

Song number three will always find the dancer with her top removed and smiling while making direct patron eye-contact to ensure a quality round of tips.

Let's talk about tips for a moment. There are men on the way up who believe it is only necessary to tip the dancers they find to be most entertaining. In general, this is a myth. If you do not tip the dancer you are probably not on the way up and are most likely cheap. At least everyone else in the bar with think you are!

The mode in which tips are collected varies widely from location to location and sometimes from girl to girl. It is most common that your female entertainer will approach you from behind and tap you on the shoulder to let you know that she is there for your moment of personal entertainment. Pragmatically, of course, you knew that she was coming, since you casually watched her movement around the bar moving from customer to customer (or from dope to dope as women outside of the profession might say.) Having notified you of her presence, she will then proceed to personally dance for you twenty or thirty seconds before presenting her lovely cleavage. At this point a man on the way up must choose to do the right thing and fill that cleavage with a dollar bill. Usually she will then dance a few more steps and present you with an opportunity to place money in her g-string in some fashion. If she is shy she will simply present you with her bosoms for a donation and head to the next guy. If she is not shy, she will accept the first dollar in her cleavage and then do a pirouette before backing into your crotch while making an appealing jiggling motion. Sometimes that pirouette routine will keep going for as long as it takes your hand to get tired making donations. It is up to you to determine where to stop this charitable appreciation process, however the first dollar is de rigueur.

Alternatively, many of these lounges focus more strongly on the female entertainment side of the equation, providing a larger number and variety of women traveling around the bar perimeter. In doing so, these bars tend to charge more for the drinks in exchange for the extra attention provided to you. It is not unusual for the more entertainment-focused bars to provide a special couch dance room with which your female companion may better concentrate on appealing to your special part. (Deep in the male southern brain, there is a mysterious longing for the couch dance room.) Depending on where the room is located, that appeal may be stronger or weaker. In more swill-oriented emporiums, the couch dance room may be plainly visible to the other patrons. It may in fact simply be a chair surrounded by a bead curtain right next to the U-shaped bar! (Nothing unusual is going to happen there for sure!) You might as well give up if that is your hope!

If the couch dance room is a separate room, (usually the size of a large bathroom) you may have some small chance that the dancer will get a little wild on your behalf. This won't usually happen, however unless she has seen you as a regular customer on a number of occasions and is sure you are not a constable! Pragmatically, however, your hopes will be dashed in any event due to the ever-vigilant bouncer who cruises back and forth in front of the open couch room doors to preclude anything significantly sexual from happening.

"Lords, Why does he do this," you ask? "What does he have against me that would make him wander back and forth as if he has nothing worthwhile to do?"

Well, the first level answer that bar management will suggest is that the bouncer provides a certain level of safety for the women. Who knows, it's possible that an aggressive male under the thrall of his thingy might force a woman to do unusual acts in a high traffic area where he will likely be recognized, caught and punished. (OK, it is possible!) However this is not the primary reason.

All exotic bars operate in someone's regional jurisdiction. It may be a township, it may be a city, it could be on an Indian reservation, who knows! But someone will want to regulate that bar. Usually in these more rural situations, it will be a town council that is concerned about the blight to the neighborhood and potential unruly customers that might be attracted. Of course we know that a man on his way up will not be unruly, but he may easily find himself among men with that reputation, such as the often-present bikers, for example.

Another ongoing concern about these bars is their ownership and financing. Although many are owned by independent entrepreneurs, quite a number are owned or funded by rather shadowy organizations such as the ones we watch cable television series about. For these organizations, it's a rather easy transition from bookmaking to working with women that may be somewhat flexible in their character while dispensing beer to customers and themselves. On the other hand, your local "club" could be run by a mom and pop team that has been there valiantly paying taxes for years. Regardless, the perceived source of ownership will typically lend some weight to the type of regulation that reflects on your bar of choice.

This regulation can occur in a number of ways. It can result in the re-zoning of neighborhoods that will suddenly make it difficult for a bar to continue to exist. It may instead result in a number of visits by the local liquor control board to make sure management is operationally talented enough to continue to utilize its expensive liquor license. And let me say that is no small threat. If an owner's liquor license is pulled and the bar goes out of business, he is Shit Out of Luck. So even honest entrepreneurs have to walk carefully to make sure they aren't prosecuted for violating local laws. And the easiest way to find a bar owner in this repressive condition is for he/she to become a little lax in oversight of the scantily clad women. Soon someone with an ax to grind will ensure that the bar receives some aggressive inspections!

To limit this possibility, the bar hires an annoying bouncer who doesn't really want to keep sticking his head through the door to watch other people's private activities (well maybe some do,) and has him peek in every once in a while to quell any inappropriate actions. The girls who engage in them will be disciplined, either by being sent home for the day or perhaps permanently.

It is not unusual for regulating entities to send in undercover policeman. They check to see if solicitation occurs in some manner or if the outfits worn by the dancers are a little too revealing, perhaps during your personal moment of entertainment around the bar. When a bar is tagged in this fashion, the owner is usually put on notice that a second offense within a certain period of time will result in a significant fine or perhaps the license being yanked. As a result, entertainment in the bar goes into a state of hibernation. Although it will continue, it will be very closely monitored and formerly friendly women will stay at arms length! Now what fun is that for a man on the way up?

Urban Exotic Bars

Exotic bars in cities operate in much the same way as in more rural regions. The primary difference is that in urban areas, the regulation may at times appear to be more relaxed. This is because city planners have more important issues to contend with. The police force needs to concentrate on more serious crime and simply keeping auto traffic flowing. Oftentimes the city community is more accepting of the existence of exotic places. Perhaps the bar will be relegated to a certain section of town. Perhaps not. Regardless, it would be a fair statement to say that with a greater concentration of population, there is a tendency for exotic bars to provide an enhanced level of entertainment.

For example, a dancer may decide that to ensure a higher level of tips during her personal dance, she may elect to lean up against your thingy during preliminary conversation (or just grind into it wildly as she backs into you). Usually this will be accompanied with the offer of a couch dance in the private room. There is, once again, something appealing about responding to a woman's offer when she is leaning against your favorite pipe. As a man on your way up, it is important, however, to realize that 95% of the time, your private couch dance is going to provide little more than a private version of the same dance you received five minutes earlier while sitting in the main bar area. Well, okay, she will likely take off her top while doing it for you. But if that bouncer is popping in and out of your line of vision (you'd like to pop him, I'm sure) you aren't going to get much more effect than if you'd kept your $20!

So what is a man on the way up to do for more entertainment? Well, first you must realize that even if you lock onto the most beautiful and willing dancer in a private room without a bouncer, you can still end up catching a dread disease that will make you wither and die in an unpleasant manner, years before it is programmed in your genetic code. So should you land in that situation, a man on the way up will not even consider male thingy to female thingy contact. It's just too dangerous. As an alternative, many men believe that in a bar they are likely to find a dancer who will be willing to provide them with oral pleasure for the $60 or $80 they are willing to offer. That may (or may not) be true, however, any woman who is willing to repeatedly do that for men they don't know is likely to end up with a withering disease as discussed earlier. It would seem inappropriate for a man on the way up to contribute to some young woman's demise from a sociological viewpoint. It would be safer, for example, if you found yourself in such an isolated situation, to simply give each other those very pleasurable and somewhat safer hand jobs!

"But Lords, you've already said that such bars hire bouncers so patrons will be encouraged to avoid such situations!"

Yes, that's absolutely true. However most exotic bars go through various cycles over time. And they implement rules that act to keep their costs down just like any other business. Many bars, for example, get sold every two or three years. When this occurs, the new management usually throws out a number of the old employees, (who they are certain are stealing money from the till) and hires new people who aren't as familiar with the ropes. During this transition period, the dancers will often find themselves with more relaxed rules that will enable them to do more to please a customer, should he offer them the appropriate incentive.

Another cycle that occurs with more regularity is simply the day-in day-out operating cycle. It is a truism that topless bars do more business during the evening. Oftentimes the day is relatively boring with dancers walking around and waiting for someone, anyone to come in. In the summer it can get even worse. People like to stay outside where it's sunny. A glance inside an exotic bar may reveal dancers dancing for each other. More often, with no customers, they will simply sit at the bar with bored expressions. Management does not like to hire bouncers to baby-sit bored women. So it is not unusual to find that the bouncer isn't on-duty during the afternoon and only shows up at 4:00 p.m. In such a situation, in an urban setting, it would not be unusual for a man on the way up to find an unusually flexible group of women to keep him company. Unless, however, you are relatively candid when each dancer decides to do her personal review, you can be sure that your private dance will be the generic dance that everyone else receives in the couch room. The bottom line here is that in the evening, the supply of cash donors is much higher and a dancer doesn't have to work as hard. In the afternoon supply is lower and the demand for customers is higher. Supply and demand come together to fill needs. This truth operates in topless bars like anywhere else!

Gentlemen's Clubs

Gentlemen's clubs are upscale topless bars. They are often larger than the less fancy places and are populated with a higher percentage of attractive women. The more standard exotic bar will usually be populated with some attractive women and a few not so attractive. If you want to see the best sights Gentlemen's Clubs are for you! The upscale value will additionally attract a higher number of women hoping to meet you for five minutes. And usually you get to see them in the presence of nice wood paneling and brass rails!

This attractive ambiance comes with a certain trade-off. In view of the expense required to purchase, staff, and maintain such a place, a large amount of cash is needed from bigger-than-average investors. As a result, these places tend to have more attention paid to them by the regulators, who automatically suspect that cash funding comes from less-than-legitimate sources. (Who knows, it may be true.) Management's concern about such investigations tends to make them stay a little more conservatively between the lines. A $20 couch dance in a place like this is going to be generic in nature. Don't even bother trying to talk a dancer into being flexible. In fact, many gentlemen's clubs do not have private couch dance rooms. Instead they may have a couch dance area where there truly is no privacy. Expect the bouncer to tell you to put your arms where he can see them. But at least the chairs or lounges will be padded and very comfortable!

It is not unusual for a place like this to have a special "champagne room" for the high roller who comes in for some drinks. Couch dances in these rooms tend to run in the $200-300 range. In theory, some private time in these rooms comes with some extra benefits. It will take that much cash to find out! Whether true or not is unclear. To protect the bar in such a case, management will likely post a bouncer to keep unexpected inspectors from just pushing their way in unannounced.

The other major trade-off in a bar like this is the price of the drinks. Given the need to pay for that fine wood paneling, you can expect the drinks to run a few dollars higher than other less-upscale bars in the area.

BYOB All Nude Bars

In a completely different class of entertainment for your thingy is the BYOB (Bring Your Own Booze) All Nude bar. Existing in areas where regular topless bars are subject to regulation by a liquor control agency, these bars get around that oversight by not offering beer or alcoholic drinks at all. Instead, they offer you the opportunity to bring your own beer (or whatever) and store it in their cooler (or even bring your own cooler for that large bachelor party.) Of course if you store it in their cooler you should tip the "bartender" for keeping your beverages cold. BYOB bars make their basic revenues by charging a per head fee when you walk through the door. It may be $15. It may be $25. They may also charge for cooling your drinks, but they definitely aren't going to make money by selling liquor.

These bars come in all sizes. The larger ones offer a limited food selection to feed your stomach cravings as you watch the beautiful sights. For a man on the way up who has never been in a place like this, you will likely experience a strange dichotomy of emotions. First you will find that there are many women who either by intrinsic nature or from experience have developed a high comfort-level while walking completely unclothed among men. From a male perspective, it is a little different from the traditional topless bar in which the dancer elects to pull down her g-string to entice your lower brain with a flash. These women, instead, have nothing on except their birthday suits and a garter for your tips.

In talking to them, you will find that many are nice girls, just like you would expect to find anywhere else. They will turn out to be students or dental assistants in their everyday lives. What you may find, however, is that the lack of clothing creates something of an informational barrier. To protect themselves, they cannot carry on in-depth conversations. And to some degree you may decide to personally refrain from asking the questions you might normally ask. It's a little strange!

These bars will also have couch dance rooms where you can get that private dance for $20-$50, depending on time spent, number of songs, etc. What you see outside of the room will, once again, reflect what goes on within. First, you aren't going to see any more skin. You can't. Second, these bars also tend to be regulated, it's just not by liquor control agencies. It would not be surprising to have an undercover cop go into one of these rooms and attempt to receive a solicitation. Hell, every other guy wants to! So if you want the intimacy that private conversation allows (within limits) feel free to drop your cash. But don't expect it to go beyond conversation. In addition, since these women feel a little more vulnerable, they may be a little skittish when your hand wanders. So be prepared to sit on them.

Triple X Establishments

I wasn't even going to bring these up but since I've gone into such detail, I might as well complete the circle. In some urban areas a man on the way up will occasionally stumble into a triple X establishment. These are the places that say "Live Nude Girls" in blinking neon on the side. Although some of the features of these places overlap with the previously-mentioned establishments, they have a certain feel to them that is their own. In large measure, these places are built to serve men who have reached a level of desperation that they wish to see a woman without clothes on and they wish to see her now and in a very sexual manner! Now I think most of us have reached that point at sometime in our lives, however not all individuals follow through on the urge. For the duration that you attend one of these places, a "man on the way up" must give up that title and put on the title "pervert." Not that there's anything wrong with that! For this period it is clear that you are close to the edge. So what happens here?

In these establishments you first get to pass all of the intricate plastic toys that are displayed on shelf after shelf for your inspection and purchase. Now personally I don't think I would find that much enjoyment by using an artificial "squeezebox" with real live feel; or plastic breasts and butt that can be worn in front of the mirror; or even an eight inch vibrating dildo with little ticklers at the end. However, given the supply available, there is clearly a group of people that enjoys these items enough to provide the demand. Their market presence is clearly visible when you walk through the turnstile. So after perusing the large variety of toys, you can amble to the next part of the room that has the all-nude strutting bar (which may be BYOB) depending on whether alcohol is allowed. In this room women of greater and lesser attractiveness will strut their stuff, either (1) on stage in front of barstools or (2) inside a closed area which forces you to go into little closets and put tokens or money into a machine to keep your window open. In this more claustrophobic gaze-a-rama, the women will often put on a show demonstrating some of the little plastic toys you saw earlier (you did want to see something resembling a live sex act didn't you?) Or if not, they will likely give you an individual view usually only seen by their gynecologists. Once again, however, you aren't touching her. If the ladies get bored with their strutting bar performances, they may sit cross-legged and allow you to crumple up dollars bills and throw them targeted to land in a most unusual spot.

After tiring of this show, you will likely stand up and get a chance to walk through private-room couchland. Typically, there will be girls standing in front of several rooms. You walk up to the one who appeals to you most, give her some nominal tip, and she will lead you inside to discuss fees for whatever may occur.

But surprise, these women are concerned about their health too. They will be happy to dance for you without clothes; climb on top of you; and in general get you all riled up. They'll even let you have an orgasm, unfortunately they want you to do the job for them. (Use your own hand.) So you haven't gained much here except an unusually clear medical view. The one good thing is if you do it yourself, you'll probably get it right!

"But Lords, Doesn't anyone ever do it for you?"

Sure. If you walk into the sleazier porno blocks in certain cities someone is going to do it for you. Prostitutes exist in all large cities. But do you really want them to? Many of these women are on crack cocaine. Many of them are on other drugs. I'm not sure even a hand job is safe! (Well, paranoia is a good thing!) You don't want to be testing the confidence limits of statistics here. And remember, when you walked into the tamer triple X establishments you already gave up the title "man on the way up." Until you leave the porno block you will still be a pervert!

General Information

"So unless I become a pervert I'm not going to get my rocks off?" Well, I really didn't say that. I think, however, it's important to have a slightly different state of mind. To enjoy the pleasures of women engaging in your own self-satisfaction, you first need to enjoy their satisfaction. You have to enjoy them. If a woman recognizes that you only see them as a means to an end, my suggestion is that you go out, get yourself a TV, and buy yourself a nice set of porno tapes. You'll be getting a lot of use out of them.

If however, you are a little less selfish, and are willing to enjoy their company and provide satisfaction to women before searching for your own, good things will begin to happen to you. First of all, it's important to show that you care about them. Of course you may not. You may for example, be some sort of sociopath. If that is the case you will have to *pretend* you care. Hopefully you will do a bad job!

Assuming however that your head is on straight, it is important to become a little less self-centered and enjoy the company of your companion. If you don't, she will recognize your selfishness and blow you off. Let me rephrase that. She will send you packing. It's probably just as well, you weren't meant to be together. Now this sounds like it applies primarily to normal relationships outside of the rather sexually-charged atmosphere that we've been discussing. And it does! But it really applies at all times. It applies to the nice girl that you met at the coffee shop and it applies to the exotic dancer walking around the bar trying to show you her wares.

I think this was another secret of my friend Perry who was always able to pick up dancers. He loved women! He loved everything about them. Their companionship, their feel, their taste, their smell, their voices, their laughter. When you love women on a number of levels, they see it and respond in kind. The difference between a conventional relationship and one inside of a topless bar is that you've already got the meeting part figured out! That attractive woman is going to walk right over and make your acquaintance unabashedly!

For the conventional relationship that you start in a normal environment, you are going to stumble into dates as part of the everyday process of interacting with friends, going to parties, and working with your peers. Your dating pool will be determined by chance meetings that occur during your daily activities. If you are looking for a long-term relationship, this is a very good thing. The success of long-term relationships is determined largely by having common interests with your mate. Great sex can work for a while, but twenty years down the road you will want to still have something to talk about and more importantly, do together. Perhaps you are both skiers. Perhaps you both like to go camping. These types of common interests can go a long way toward planning symbiotic lives. In your own self-interest, try not to hook up with people who have a world view in direct conflict with your own. Your statistical odds of success are lower. You may stay together but your life's enjoyment will be decreased. If you are not sure what I'm talking about read Romeo and Juliet. Or look at the tension that occurs when you herd a number of Palestinians into the same room with a bunch of Israelis!

After interacting through the dating process, you will winnow through some potential mates. You may do all sorts of activities. You may simply take them out to dinner. It's a process that develops over time. At some point you are will end up in a sexually intimate situation in which you will either demonstrate your caring or that you are a "me first" kind of guy. Should this lack of mutual sharing occur, you will likely begin your dating process again. If not, you will continue to develop your intimate relationship for as long as the two of you interact together.

What I have described for you is a process that requires chance meetings; occurs over weeks or months; and can fall apart before any intimate opportunity ever occurs. It is an investment in time and resources on your part in the meeting of a potential life mate. If you view intimacy as the payoff here, (and it really shouldn't be, instead it should be the identification of a life mate with intimacy as a side benefit,) then you've achieved it. It just took a long period of time.

A person in a topless bar, if not simply enjoying a cursory eye-candy thrill, is looking for intimacy on a much shorter time schedule. Well here is some good news! The feedback loop is a lot shorter in this environment. You get to skip the part where you accidentally run into your friend for the first time; you don't have to have any preliminary discussions that determine if you have any common interests; you don't have to buy her dinner or take her to any movies; you will, however, face many of the same barriers to intimacy that happen with everyone else.

But first, you have to face those physical barriers again. Nothing is going to happen in a bar unless there is a private room somewhere. Okay, let's clarify, semi-private room. These rooms, as noted before, do not usually have doors!

Let's hypothesize that you have noted that during the day, no bouncer frequents the stool near the couch dance room to interrupt your activities.

"So the dancer comes over, asks if you want a couch dance, you nod your head and go back to the couch dance room, right?" Wrong, you've already blown it. At this point you are assured to receive the generic couch dance that applies to the general public. Before any of this happens, the enchantress will come over to dance for you and receive your token tips. If you stiff her in any way you're not going to get very far. Cheap is not a prized personality trait in men.

In a topless bar, stupidity in men *is* actually prized but stupidity is defined as ordering countless generic couch dances!

Usually at some point during your several minutes of entertainment, the lady will engage you in some form of light conversation. She's actually doing the same thing you are, except for another reason. She wants to see if you are a relatively sane individual and if you are likely to have some interest in a generic couch dance. Mentally unstable people, if identified, will not receive an inquiry. This is how she makes most of the money to pay her rent. If she only walks through the bar patrons and accepts nominal tips after her hourly turn on stage she may only make $20 for that period. These are not women who work eight hours a day. Their shift may be four hours. They may have to split tips with the bouncer or bartender. On a warm summer day, the afternoon bar may be completely deserted and no money gets made. So she is anxious to have you go to the back and drop $20-$60 on her for food money!

If at this point you treat her as a piece of meat (and assuming you are mentally sound) she will still take you back to that room and flounce around all over you. If you happen to have a hair trigger for flouncers you are in luck! Unfortunately, there is a bad side for a man on the way up in this case. He will have to walk around with saturated underwear. Yuck!

Most men on the way up do not really want to have an orgasm in their pants. So be forewarned, perhaps if this is you, it would be a good idea to stick some napkins or tissues in your pocket before you ever get to the location. But let's go back to your mistake!

Instead of treating her like a piece of meat, you decide to enjoy her company without exhibiting any tendencies that suggest the last dollar you gave her blew your allowance and you won't be getting any more from your parents this month. So you talk to her for a while, (she probably is cute) and she sizes you up at the same time. Soon she brings the conversation around to inquire if you are interested in a private couch dance in the back room. Well of course you are. Who wouldn't be? But before you take that walk, there has to be an understanding that one of you will have an orgasm. And you may have to explain that you mean a hand job here. No one in their right mind would expect to have sex with someone they don't really know who works in such an establishment. It would simply be too dangerous.

Now back to the orgasmic proposition. It accomplishes a couple of things. First of all, this will send away a large proportion of the dancers without much further discussion. They may shake their heads when they walk away, however you have winnowed down the crowd. A new woman will shortly come along and you can determine her flexibility at that time.

"Why," you ask, "Did I tell her that either of us could have the orgasm?" Well, if you enjoy a woman's pleasure, it shouldn't matter too much whether it is you or her. The enjoyment she exudes as you provide a power orgasm from the vertical couch dance position will probably be worth a couple of couch dances. (Once again, you have to be in shape and have arm strength to do this.) You won't get much chance to lie down in a couch room. And if a woman allows you to give her an orgasm, at some point she is going to reciprocate. It may not be today but it will happen a week or two later.

The other side of the coin is that she may prefer to give you the orgasm. Many women in this situation feel that anything invasive is exactly that. It may be a matter of minimizing their health risk, or it may simply be too personal. Or it may simply be more fun for them, who knows. Once again, if you go back to a couch room under these conditions, bring a few tissues or prepare to be soggy.

For the record, it is not unusual for a woman to say she is okay with the proposition but then have second thoughts when she gets back there. When it is clear she is just going to flounce around on you for three minutes, stop at the end of dance number one and pay your $20 and leave.

"What about oral sex?" Well, admittedly this is a book about your thingy and some of the pleasures it may experience. But the reality is, even if you find a dancer willing to provide oral sex, you just shouldn't. Your risk of catching HIV will probably be low, however you will be encouraging activities that may get your friend (and you need to care a little here) killed or sick in the long run. Although the occurrences are low, repetitive oral sex activities amongst a wide population of partners can result in an HIV/AIDS transmission. It just takes the wrong one and some bad luck! In addition, these activities will likely result in the transmission of more infectious diseases like syphilis or gonorrhea. Don't encourage this activity with someone who is likely to do it more often as a result. It's simply wrong!

CHAPTER 8

Your Part and Protective Apparel

"Lords. In the twenty-first century, how can a man on the way up protect himself against the myriad health issues he might face on the sexual landscape?" This, of course, is one of the primary questions we must address in order to survive long enough to reach our genetic-code-determined age of departure. Now some of us believe that success at living doesn't actually require us to hit the point of decrepit senility. The quality of life achieved beyond one's 80's doesn't always argue for allowing your tissue to age and wear until the last possible moment of consciousness. There are some quite convincing arguments for euthanasia in a number of circumstances. If you are no longer able to recognize visitors who come into your ward, or if you are in constant pain, why hang out? Let go and move on. Maybe there *is* an afterlife! But if you haven't reached that point, recognize that you will still be able to have some fun as long as your personal snake is operative. So it's clearly not advisable to take chances that will cut short your functional life by 30 or 40 years. That brings us to our next topic of *protective apparel*.

For those of us who are extremely paranoid, an appropriate choice of everyday wear would be a full-body protective coat of latex, painted on to cover everything, with the possible exception of eye and nostril holes. Unfortunately that doesn't recognize the fact that we still have to eliminate body wastes of one kind or another, so with a few extra holes, there goes our protection! Then of course we will find that some individuals are allergic to latex, making it impractical for them. Then no doubt we will find that you really can't paint a person with a protective layer to stop all possible germ penetrations. Remember, it was enough to kill the girl in "Goldfinger."

More problematic is the fact that a sheer, full-body coat of latex is not a good fashion statement. When everyone walking in the streets is covered by a thin layer of glop, we tend to lose our individuality. In the fashion world, individuality is extremely important. Sure, we can have red glop and green glop, but in the final analysis it's still glop. It smoothes over the details making us all look alike. Since it won't pass muster with the fashion police, we are left with germ protection levels that will be less than fully effective and will require us to use an on again/off again approach. There won't be any full-time, always-on protective apparel.

"So how does one protect himself against the various germs and creatures that are trying to kill us, or at least screw things up?" Well, there are a number of levels of protection that we can talk about. Take a look at the items below:

Abstinence

I put this in so that this book would get the seal of approval of the conservative religious right-wing establishment. Now I've never been exactly sure what this means so I'm going to hypothesize a couple of possibilities.

Number 1: This means that you try not to think about sex and never touch yourself in a way that might cause you to think about sex. Consequently, you never really get around to having sex in any flavor. If you can do this you should be safe. There are, however, a couple of problems that may present themselves. First of all you may be walking down the street and see a woman. This may cause you to think about sex. You may decide to divert your attention onto other matters, such as cloud-watching. This may hold your attention until two large and puffy clouds come together and look like two enormous boobs. This may cause you to think about sex. My thought here is that it is difficult not to think about sex on a fairly regular basis. Nonetheless, the requirement is to not think about sex, thus minimizing your desires. And then if you do think about sex you must refrain from taking action. This second part is really pretty difficult. I think it may be easier to do the second part if you are actually pretty religious in character (or at least have a large religious-type guilt complex.) Whether you want sex or not, you may find yourself refraining from having any if you think some omnipotent old guy is looking over your shoulder from the clouds above (the ones with the big boobs in them.)

Number 2: In the second definition of abstinence you are allowed to think about sex, you're just not allowed to have any with anyone but yourself. A corollary of this approach is that you may be able to control some of that desire by constantly masturbating to take the edge off. Think about it, you're walking around at that pool party with all of your peers and female friends (who happen to be in bathing suits) and you suddenly get an erection. Rather than embarrass yourself, you just duck behind the nearest tree and choke your weasel until the urge is expunged. Given the typical male need to recover from orgasm for a period of time, this approach may work to quell your imminent sexual desires. Just remember that your acquaintances may start to ask where you're always popping off to and why you always come back with tree bark stuck to your shirt. Once again, this is another argument for a man on the way up to carry those little packets of tissue. Make sure you track the direction of all of those orgasmic blasts or you may look down at your trousers and find you are carrying some sticky ballast that you didn't expect anyone to see.

Now I'm going to point out that it is very important for a man on the way up to camouflage this activity while in public places. I used to attend the local YMCA a number of years ago. I would run or work out or do some other form of physical exercise. Once after one of those workouts I jumped in the shower (as usual—not the only time I ever did it) and turned on my particular shower-head, one among many in the public male locker room. It was not crowded that day. At the time it appeared there was only one other person taking a shower. He wasn't real obvious because there was a lot of steam in the room; and he was standing behind a big steel support beam that happened to run straight down through the shower room ceiling. I didn't give it a lot of thought until I looked out of the corner of my eye a few minutes later and although I couldn't really see him, I could see his hand. And his hand was going up and down rather methodically!

Now I suppose I should have taken that as a compliment. I was, of course, the only other guy in the shower and buck-naked to boot. It's 95% certain that he was focused on me. And not that there's anything wrong with that, but I don't happen to ebb and flow in that direction. I felt that I was not the appropriate person to be the object of that individual's mental stimulation. And I would like to point out that if you get caught taking this action in public you are no longer "a man on the way up." You have, once again released this title in order that it may be replaced by the "pervert" title. And it's hard to get rid of that pervert title. It tends to be sticky throughout your career.

Back to the topic at hand. The good thing about abstinence is that from a disease perspective, it is perfectly safe. If you stay away from everyone you will not be able to pass or receive any sexually transmitted diseases. The bad thing is that many individuals do not have the will-power to pull it off. For those that cannot, we have the next layer of protection which is:

Restrictive Behavior

A man on the way up will not always have perfect knowledge of his companion's health history. Even if his companion swears she is a virgin there is a strong chance that she has been intimate with a number of companions. There's no great payoff for a woman to advertise that she has been around the block a number of times. So to protect himself, a man on the way up must assume his friend is bending the facts. Using this philosophy to minimize exposure, the number of activities that may be engaged in is limited.

The first, and prime restriction is to limit yourself to hand jobs. If you are providing your companion with a manual orgasm, make sure that you have no cuts, scratches, sores, bleeding hangnails, or other conditions that could allow your companion's body fluids to mix with your own internally. The skin is reputed to be a pretty strong barrier to infection as long as it is not broken. After you have pleasured her, it is recommended you wash your hands to minimize the time that any body fluids might settle under your fingernails or on your skin. If she is manually giving you orgasms, thank your lucky stars. There's nothing like a good orgasm! But first make sure she starts out with clean hands. If you have ferreted out dancers, for example, who are flexible with their couch dance customers, you should assume that you are not the only one. Dancer's reputations will ultimately get around. You do not want her rubbing the last customer's "cum" on your thingy because she didn't find the time to wash her hands. It seems like a small likelihood but it could happen. Assuming she engages in a straight hand job, with cleanliness, it will be difficult for any body-fluid-related diseases to be spread.

If someone is grinding a couch dance on you at the same time, it is also possible that she could be spreading little pubic-hair gremlins (lice) that may not be lethal, but may cause you some future embarrassment. That danger occurs during any couch dance in which the customer's pants have somehow come open.

And now for a slight departure of topic. You will occasionally find a bar in which the couch dance room is closely watched but the activities around the beverage serving area are not. Some women looking for tips will allow you to insert your fingers into *their* thingys to try and encourage you into that heavily monitored couch dance. If you engage in this with one girl and then another similarly flexible girl walks up, you could be spreading body fluids from one girl to the next. Many girls in these places never consider that possibility. If you engage in that activity, make sure you either wash your hands between such events, or at least don't use the same hand until you cleaned it. Remember we actually like these girls, we don't want them to get hurt! Staying in this mindset for a moment, you will occasionally find a dancer who doesn't mind giving her customers oral sex. Although it doesn't present a high probability of passing an automatically lethal disease (i.e., HIV/AIDS) to you, in the long run this pattern may create other STD health issues for them or you. (Okay, I'm repeating myself here.)

Then there is the other side of the coin. You will occasionally find dancers that would not mind if you were to perform oral sex on them. Certainly it is a low risk issue for the woman. I would suggest however, that it is not a good idea. If she has a disease, the possibility exists that it could be transferred into a cut or the membranes of your mouth. The more infectious diseases like herpes, hepatitis B, gonorrhea, warts and syphilis would have a higher probability here.

Leaving the exotic bar scene again, the next level of protection relates to:

Condoms

If neither abstinence nor hand jobs are going to take care of you, you have now reached the point where you need to be carrying and using latex condoms. It doesn't matter where you are or whom you are with, any individual that you don't know in a day-to-day monogamous relationship should be treated as if she has the possibility of carrying a disease. She might very well not know it!

If it is in your plan to insert your thingy in any of a woman's lower orifices, you need to pull out one of these and put in on your organ before it starts to get out of control. Pragmatically, in order to prevent pregnancy, you should put one on before it gets near your friend's body. Rather than treat it as a necessary evil, you should think of it as a fashion statement. If you walk into your pharmacy and check out the selection, you will find that they have big ones, medium ones (I don't think I've seen any with the words "small" on them [since no one would buy them]) colored ones, textured ones, and ones with little feelers on the end. This is your opportunity to give yourself a certain sense of style. Convey that fashion sense when you put it on, rather than the need to have protection against disease! If you don't, you are risking an unnatural shortening of your life that you will regret. It's one thing to blow off the possibility of disease and say "if I catch it I'll take my medicine and not complain." It's another thing when reality hits, you are constantly in pain, physically scarred, and withering away without any friends. Keep that possibility a little closer to the front of your mind so you'll be more likely to do the right thing!

Just open your condom up, make sure it's unrolling in the right direction, and slide it down your Johnson. Just think of the mental stress you'll be avoiding when you find out that "nice" girl was nice to everyone else that you know. By the way, condoms fail a small percentage of the time. They're not foolproof.

One other comment. Some individuals are allergic to latex condoms. In that eventuality, polyurethane (plastic) condoms are the fall-back choice. Both of these types have been shown to protect against HIV. Some of the natural membrane condoms have failed the HIV protection test. Don't take a chance here.

Lubrication

Any time you contemplate sticking your guy where the "sun don't shine", you need to be concerned about lubrication. (Okay, if that metaphor was lost on you, we're talking about anal sex here.) First, that particular passageway was generally made to go in one direction. It's an exit, not an entrance. When you wheel your machine up behind it, you're swimming upstream. Second, it's a fairly small stream and a relatively large boat. So when you're cruising upstream, it's likely that you're going to be squeezing up against the bank and taking a few chunks off it.

Perhaps I should be more direct here. Without adequate lubrication, [and don't forget that condom] your partner may feel quite uncomfortable when you stick your tool inside. She (or he, not that there's anything wrong with that) will need to be relaxing her gate just to allow you to get through. Once inside, lubrication should help avoid other potential issues that might occur. Simply sticking something that big in a space that tight can result in disruptions to the internal tissues that make it more likely to pass diseases that we don't even want to think about. And who wants dry sex anyhow? If you think you might prefer it this way, make sure you ask for your next colonoscopy without any lubricating aids. Your doctor will think you're a hero for keeping down the soaring cost of healthcare!

If on the other hand you prefer things to be pleasurable, go down to your local pharmacy and purchase your favorite brand of water-based lubricant. It doesn't cost much and it will ease the situation considerably. Oil-based lubricants like petroleum jelly and baby oil can dissolve the chemical structure of the latex condom so stay away from them. Most individuals prefer their condoms without holes according to a recent internet poll. KY Jelly is water-based so you can use their products. By the way, on this particular topic, it's not uncommon for some women to aid in the stimulation of your particular thingy in the somewhat kinky fashion of sticking one of her fingers inside your anus (you know, your ass). Well that's great. I like someone who's adventuresome. I would point out however that many women have long fingernails that are almost like little knives. I would suggest therefore that any woman doing this consider, once again, grabbing a jar of some water-based lubricant like KY Jelly and oiling up her finger before she does damage to her man. Just repeat this mantra if you forget. "Sex and Freddy Krueger don't mix—Sex and Freddy Krueger don't mix."

Pregnancy Protection

Another thing that works pretty well for avoiding pregnancy is a vasectomy. It's generally a one-time solution, (you don't want to go around reversing these things) that will effectively put an end to your fathering capabilities. For a man on the way up though, it may be a little pre-mature to be tying off your shoelaces. Give yourself at least ten years or so of post-adolescent sexuality before making this permanent commitment. If you think about it, you're likely to be wearing condoms anyhow just to avoid various diseases. So the pregnancy concern is a non-issue without having to do anything at all! Of course if you happen to know that your sociopathic tendencies are genetic in character, feel free to pull the plug at an early age. You'll be doing us all a favor.

Things that don't work very well

Masks—Why the hell would you wear a mask? Are you one of those guys whom jumps out of the bushes? Or just scared that someone will spit on you? Unless you are trying to protect your anonymity, you won't find this very helpful. In fact you are more likely to scare your partner than anything else. Of course they do sell all sorts of leather things including masks at your local kinky sex shop. It's worth a trip down there just to see what they have.

Even if you aren't particularly comfortable in your leather pants and leather cycle jacket, it should make for some great pictures as you stand next to your friend in a leather halter and mini-skirt wearing her combination leather thong and black fishnet stockings. Actually that might look pretty impressive! Get a good Nikon or one of the more recent digital cameras and snap away! You won't have to take that digital camera to a store to get it developed, just download it on your computer. You're on your own. Gee, you'll find that restrictive won't you! An attractive semi-clothed companion with no fashion inhibitions together with you and your camera. This is what America is all about. And certainly worth defending I might add.

Enlargement Cream

Is there any kind of cream that doesn't enlarge your penis if you rub some on it? Perhaps itching powder cream won't. I would say that for the vast majority of men, rubbing any other cream on your penis will, in fact, add a couple of inches onto what was hanging out there in the beginning. Just bear in mind that the increase will likely diminish a few minutes later when you stop rubbing.

On the other side, this could be fun if you can convince your partner of the need to check out these various forms of cream. Maybe you can find some that are flavored!

Rubber Tits and Asses

Well, you find these in a lot of stores. You know, the big rubber boobs you can put on and the giant rubber ass to strap on . . . well your ass. These are probably meant to be Halloween items more than anything else. But who knows, maybe they are useful. I suppose if you stick on one of those rubber asses you'll find yourself protected from anyone considering your personal rear entry. I'm told these are hot sellers in the prison commissary.

Something That Does Work

If you find that your personal tool isn't getting enough attention and you've tried some of the ideas in prior chapters without success, perhaps it's time to sit back and evaluate how you look and interact with people. First of all, women really like someone who can make them laugh. If you want to have a lot of friends, female or otherwise, brush up on your sense of humor.

And in that more shallower of realities, looks do count! If you are one of those guys who returns for dinner seconds on a regular basis and has developed a gut, this is definitely not a plus in the area of relationships. In the same way men have an internalized primal desire for curvaceous female creatures, women have a similar primal desire for V-shaped men. That is, your top should be relatively muscular and broad compared to your gut. To allow your body to eat itself into the opposite position will degrade your ability to attract the opposite sex. In addition, it will cause your own confidence level to decrease (which will likely cause you to sit at home and eat more.)

The good news is that you can do something about it. Those pictures that you see in books about people who have morphed their bodies from relatively non-muscular body shapes into trim beautiful people are true. All it takes is a decision on your part to change your body shape and the decisiveness to stick to your plan. If you make the plan your main priority you will succeed. If you let everything else get in the way then you will fail. It's as simple as that.

To make this work will entail changing your diet from one in which you chow down huge quantities of food two or three times a day, to one in which you consume six small meals containing lots of protein but relatively few fats and carbohydrates. By controlling your diet in this fashion, you will benefit in a couple of ways: First you will eat fewer unnecessary calories. You will avoid stretching your stomach with bigger and bigger meals. And in addition, you will put in place the protein diet that will allow your exercise program to take hold.

You can shrink your body simply by taking the approach mentioned above without exercising. However if you start with a huge body lacking in muscle and then go on a diet, you will end with a smaller body lacking in muscle and tone. That is, a big potato will end up looking like a small potato. Moreover, if you start with a really big body you may end up with loose skin. You'll be healthier but still look odd. Not quite what you were aiming at!

So to end up with that V-shape, you are going to need to commit to an exercise program. The exercise should include both weight lifting to build up muscle, (you know, bench presses, arm and leg curls, push ups, sit-ups, that kind of stuff) and cardio-related exercise to burn off the extra calories. Your cardio can be running (get a good pair of running shoes) or simply using some sort of cycling machine. The important thing is to get on a regular day-in/day-out exercise schedule and stick to it. Don't let anything get in your way. I could go into a lot of detail here but it doesn't make sense. There are some very good books on the topic that will put you in great shape in no time, as long as you have the desire. Try "Body for Life" by Bill Phillips.

Once you put your body in great shape you will notice a mental morphing effect to go with the physical improvement. Your confidence will rise. And your thingy will get more attention too.

CHAPTER 9

Your Part and Pharmaceuticals

"Lords, What pharmaceuticals should I be taking to enhance my sexual experiences?"
Well the quick answer would be that a man on the way up should be ignoring any drug-related experiences to the degree possible. Why mess with success when an orgasm is a great thing to enjoy and behold. But then we must recognize that not everyone can enjoy one of these without some medical supplementation. For various medical and psychological reasons, there is a certain group of men that find it difficult to achieve or maintain an erection to the level necessary to perform sexual favors or achieve orgasms for themselves. From a male perspective this is really a drag. After hearing complaints on this topic for many years, pharmaceutical companies have finally invented something useful to address this issue.

For some portion of the men facing issues related to impotence, the drug Viagra, and similar drugs such as Levitra and Cialis can make a difference by increasing the flow of blood to your special part. In doing so, it will give your part that extra "sproing" that it needs to be functional. For a person who has been missing that sproing, this is a helping hand indeed. Imagine that you can suddenly perform sexually for that loved one after being notably absent from the game. This can and does put a smile on the faces of quite a few couples. Like many other pharmaceuticals, they are usually prescribed by a doctor unless someone is slipping you the black market variety.

Think about it though. A drug that can dramatically alter your blood flow needs to build up a safety record before being offered over the counter. So even if an informal supply is available without going to a doctor, you might want to reconsider. Also keep in mind that a lot of drugs with similar sounding names are sold on the internet to trap the unwary consumer, but generally they are just useless herbal concoctions.

In general, most men on the way up do not need the benefits of blood flow enhancers. As men grow older, the likelihood of enhancers becoming helpful will increase. So you young guys in good health shouldn't bother with unnecessary stimulation. Just get it the old-fashioned way. Remember you don't want to learn to rely on a drug early in your career. You may really need it later!

Anecdotally, we've all heard stories of young guys popping these pills and finding it hard to walk around for the next few hours without embarrassing themselves. Doubtless the circumstance will (if it hasn't already) show up in a movie since physical comedy always gets a good laugh. Do yourself a favor though and wait till you need them. If you're lucky you never will!

Other Drugs that may Work

Well of course there is always the "Morning After Pill for Men." Imagine. You have a tryst with a woman that seemed to go quite well until you wake up and realize you didn't use protection. Who knows what you might have caught? And you may have made her pregnant! That can give a man quite a headache!

Well for the headache, there may be an answer. Your favorite brand of acetaminophen or aspirin will likely make your head feel better. But for your level of stress from the prior evening there's really not much to be done. You've already shot your wad. If there's anyone who might be able to do something, it's the woman you're now too scared to call! Did you really think you could take a pill that would affect *her* after-the-fact? Come On. I told you not to be taking chances without protection! Next time use more common sense.

Other Drugs to Avoid

There are of course many drugs to be avoided for a man on the way up. In addition to the fact that they are illegal and a danger to your career, they have some bad side effects. Some of them are extremely addictive and will ruin your personality and ability to socialize on a normal basis. Take crack cocaine for example. Well don't really take it. Otherwise you can forget about being a man on the way up. Heroin may have a similar impact. Stay away from the hard stuff not only for the addiction impact but also because it will destroy your inhibitions.

On drugs like these, it is likely that when you have a sexual experience, you will not have the least concern about whom you're doing it with or with the likely health consequences. There are some urban areas (and rural I suppose) where women will simply walk up on the street and offer oral sex (or any sex you can think of) for the price of her next crack hit. It doesn't take a brain surgeon to realize she has placed herself in an extremely lethal situation. She simply won't be thinking about HIV/AIDS.

Now imagine yourself like that.

Exactly like that. Imagine yourself walking up a street and offering to service a man for your next crack hit. The urge may be so strong that you will be "doing" other men in whatever fashion they want in order to get that next high. You won't find many women willing to pay you $10 for your services. You'll be just another derelict they cross the street to avoid. Soon you'll be looking to make that quick payoff anyway you can. So unless you're just dying to catch AIDS, this isn't a good fit for your plans. Of course you can always hide behind dark corners and rob unsuspecting individuals that happen to pass by. Then you won't have to hide your new sexuality. You'll become a boy-toy for someone in a prison cell.

And on that note, so ends the cumulative wisdom of a guy who has been living with one of these parts for about 50 years. As I'm sitting on a train in the station waiting to pull out, I'm gazing at a woman on the platform with a nice shape and beautiful face. How appealing! But of course it wouldn't make sense to take major chances. I would need to know her first before doing anything rash. We don't want to be regretting an impulse that can't be reversed. As you know by now, much of becoming and remaining a man on the way up requires calming our lower brain activity when inspired by the presence of someone attractive or exciting. We need to avoid unsafe activities. Take for example the unsafe behavior demonstrated in our experiment in Chapter 2 in which the male sample population's thingys were conversing. This was followed by unexpected brain spewing behavior before departing through the back exit. Not all of this reflected safe behavior. Well of course they were conversing! It was San Francisco. Not that there's anything wrong with that. Perhaps that's why it seemed that their thingys were slightly larger than the aforementioned 15.24 centimeter standard (six inches.) In fact if one theorized that becoming gay was (at least partially) a learned behavior relating to one's first sexual experience, it seems likely that those locker room neophytes with unusually large ones would tend to receive the most attention from the alternately-oriented crowd. This would result in a predominance of "larger" males being introduced into the gay lifestyle. We could test this hypothesis with a large enough sample. We would compare the size of those following the more popular hetero lifestyle versus those following the avant-garde approach to see if there was a statistically valid size difference supporting the theory. They would have to be metrically measured of course! But enough of that. Before I let you go, I think you need some basic factual information on the topic of sexually transmitted diseases. So I've compiled some information for you and called them the "serious pages." Do yourself a favor and take the time to read them.

CHAPTER 10

The Serious Pages

Although my intent in writing this book is to provide basic guidance in the operation and maintenance of your thingy, I also wish to make it entertaining for your reading pleasure. However there are certain aspects of sexually transmitted diseases that are clinical in nature and surprise, should not be considered amusing! I think it is important however that these be communicated to you. So I am going to run through some of the more explicit facts of transmission and relative risks of some of these diseases, in particular the plague of our time, HIV/AIDS. (Well you wanted them didn't you?)

HIV/AIDS—Human Immunodeficiency Virus (HIV), which is the precursor to Acquired Immunodeficiency Syndrome (AIDS), can only be spread through one basic process, the exchange of body fluids. Now the body fluids that are known to carry the HIV virus include:

Seminal Fluid—The fluid emitted from your thingy before male orgasm.
Semen—The fluid and sperm emitted during male orgasm.

Vaginal Fluid—The fluid naturally occurring inside and prominently around a woman's vagina during sexual arousal.
Blood—The blood throughout the body of an infected person.
Breast Milk—The milk of an expecting or nursing mother who is infected.

How are these body fluids exchanged?

- Through sex.
- Through absorption through the mucous membranes such as the urethra, lining of the vagina, eyes, nose or mouth.
- Through cuts or breaks in the skin.
- From a pregnant mother to her child pre-birth or through breast milk after birth.
- From a sharing of needles between an individual who has the disease and one who doesn't.

Through sex

All sexual acts except for solo masturbation (which is different from mutual masturbation) contain some risk of exchanging body fluids. Some more than others. Let's walk through the specific risks of each.

Traditional male-female sex (missionary style for example.)

The risk to the female in this example is that an infected male will ejaculate infected seminal fluid or semen into the woman's vagina where it will sit until it is absorbed either through the mucous membranes inside or through cuts on the wall lining that may have occurred either through abrasive actions received during the sexual act or for some unrelated medical condition.

The risk to the male in this situation is that the infected woman's vaginal fluid will be absorbed through the mucous membranes in the tip of his thingy (you know, where you pee) or through an abrasion or cut of some type on the shaft of his thingy. [HIS PENIS! Gee I have to get so specific here!] So YES, a man can get HIV from an infected woman during traditional sex, not just the other way around!

Related Issues

Can't this risk be eliminated through the use of a condom? First you have to make sure that you put the condom on without getting your fluids on the outside before insertion. This requires a bit of care. Second there are some situations in which it is advisable to put lubrication on a condom. However, there can be problems. Generally, oil-based lubrications such as petroleum jelly or cooking oils should not be used. They tend to chemically break down a latex condom, making it useless. Let's face it, a condom with holes in it is not much good. The answer to this particular issue is to use water-based lubricants such as KY Jelly. They will not harm the latex from a chemical viewpoint.

What about Nonoxyl-9, shouldn't your condom be protected with this chemical? Current wisdom suggests that Nonoxyl-9 does not add any protection against HIV. It is, instead, a spermacide that may help avoid pregnancy. Some studies have suggested that Nonoxl-9 may increase vulnerability to HIV. So don't rely on this chemical to protect you from HIV. But for god's sake use a condom!

Should a woman douche in order to kill bacteria in her vagina before a sexual encounter? Current thinking suggests that the natural bacteria and fluids inside of her may act as an initial barrier to HIV that would enter with the semen or seminal fluid. By douching, a woman would be washing away some of her natural barrier and making herself more vulnerable.

Oral Sex

Now this is a question that has intrigued a lot of men. Is it possible to get HIV from oral sex? Of course there are two sides to this question. The first applies to *the person performing the oral sex* with her (or his) mouth. If you stick your tongue in an infected woman's vagina so that it can transfer fluids to your mouth or (for our women and gay readers) if you should happen to have an infected man's thingy inside of your mouth, you will be transferring some of that infection to the mucous membranes inside. It can be absorbed to a greater or lesser degree, depending on certain factors: First is the concentration and amount of the viral infection transferred over. Second is the potential for the virus to be absorbed inside the mouth. Certain activities will increase that potential. For example, if you brush your teeth and floss your gums right before performing oral sex on someone, you will have irritated and pulled some gums back from the teeth creating more likelihood that the virus can sink into an area where it can be absorbed. So brushing and flossing in the hour preceding oral sex is a bad idea. In addition, the longer the period in which dangerous fluids stay in your mouth, the higher is the probability that the virus will be absorbed. So don't be swigging those fluids around in your mouth like a wine-tasting event, either spit them out or swallow them, where stomach acids may offer a less hospitable environment. In addition, deep throating a man's thingy may remove some natural protective barriers in the mouth as it rubs the back of the mouth or throat. Another concern is that some individuals naturally get canker sores in their mouths from eating citrus fruits when in-season. Sores of this and other types offer methods for viruses to break into the body.

Similarly, individuals with gum diseases may find that gums receding from the teeth will be more vulnerable to potential invasion by the virus. So one should keep his (or her) teeth in shape, just don't do it right before the event.

Part two of our analysis is the vulnerability of individuals *receiving oral sex*. One might think that a person receiving oral sex would be perfectly safe. However it *is possible* to catch HIV while receiving oral sex. For a male, this might occur if he had cuts or sores on his thingy and the infected individual performing the act were to have gums that were bleeding due to poor dental hygiene or other mouth problems. This could also occur if a man was being deep throated while the mucous membrane tip of his thingy were to rub against an irritated portion of the other person's mouth (e.g, due to abrasions.) So it's not common but it's possible. Obviously the use of a condom (or plastic food wrap/dental dam barrier for women receiving oral sex) in this situation will reduce a lot of risk here.

When HIV is evaluated from a risk viewpoint, both providing and receiving oral sex is considered substantially less risky than either traditional sex or—

Anal Sex

Anal sex is intuitively the most likely sexual act to result in the transmission of HIV. When a man's thingy is stuck into someone else's ass, abrasive activity results. It is very likely that small tears will result in the wall of the receiver's rectum. Blood and body fluids can flow both in and out of those micro-tears. If a male has an orgasm inside the rectum of a woman (or man), there is little for that semen to do except sit around and try to be absorbed in the surrounding wall. It's not going to go anywhere on its own. This is almost like forced absorption of body fluids. First the process creates weaknesses in tissue walls and then the circumstance enhances absorption. Thus the receiver is at great risk. The "pitcher" is also at some extra risk. His thingy may receive some abrasions in the process and any blood that leaks onto him from tears in the receiver's rectum will have little place to go except be squeezed onto his thingy during the act. If you are not in a long-time monogamous relationship with someone, you do not want to be doing this. And if you do anyhow, wear a condom. It's likely to save your life.

Related Notes

Licking someone's Ass crack. (Also known as "rimming.")
This is something that is not likely to spread HIV but provides a medium to catch other diseases instead, such as herpes, gonorrhea, hepatitis B, genital warts or syphilis.

Sucking/Licking Breast Milk from a lactating woman
Although this may not be sex in the strictest sense, (it certainly registers on the kinky index) it does reflect an exchange of potentially dangerous body fluids. It is possible to catch HIV in this fashion. Do yourself a favor and try not to pick up pregnant or recently delivered women for one-night stands.

As mentioned above, a pregnant woman may pass HIV to her child while being held in the womb. This probability is reduced if the woman is medically treated with HIV-retarding drugs during pregnancy.

Although not a sex issue, it is of course important not to share any needles for any reason.
When an infected person injects himself with illegal drugs (or even if an MD injects him with a legal prescription drug,) that needle

has just become a weapon. It should be immediately disposed of in a safe manner. If instead it is picked up and used by another drug user (or accidentally pricks the skin of a nearby medical practitioner) it may well result in the spread of HIV. Do Not Share Needles—EVER.

Diagnosis

To diagnose HIV will require a test for HIV antibodies. It may not provide an accurate reading until the infection has existed for three or more months. This period is long enough for most infected individuals to develop a detectable level of antibodies in their blood. Occasionally it may take a little longer (e.g. six months) to provide for an accurate reading.

Because HIV/AIDS is a relatively recent disease and is *generally* fatal, we tend to ignore the other sexually transmitted diseases getting less publicity. (A few people with AIDS get hit by cars or die in skiing accidents, etc. It is also possible that with life expanding drugs, certain individuals who acquired the disease later in life may die of normal old-age reasons before AIDS-related conditions kill them.) Nonetheless other sexually transmitted diseases exist and are dangerous or can be fatal. Let's broaden our horizon for the moment.

SYPHILIS

Syphilis is an infection caused by bacteria (Treponema Pallidum). The disease evolves in stages. Generally it can be cured by penicillin, however if left untreated, can result in nervous disorders, paralysis, insanity and death.

Syphilis is transmitted by:

- Passing the bacteria through mucous membranes or skin abrasions.
- Spreading the bacteria from lesions or syphilitic warts, which occur on infected individuals as the disease progresses. These lesions and warts contain a high concentration of the bacteria making it easy for the disease to spread.
- After passing into the body, the bacteria enter the bloodstream and become attached to cells, causing damage to various organs.

- The disease can also be passed from a pregnant mother to her child.

Stages of the disease
- In the initial stage of the disease an infected individual will usually experience a red oval "chancre" sore at the infection site in the first 5 to 90 days. This often painless sore will appear on or around the genitals or rectum and occasionally on the mouth. Whether treated or not, the sore will disappear in approximately one to five weeks.
- In the second stage, which develops roughly one-half month to 6 and one-half months after infection, reddish-brown rashes will appear on parts of the body including the feet or hands, head or torso. So if you shake hands with a person in this stage and you happen to have a cut in your hand or you wipe your eyes, it's communicable. In addition, syphilitic warts or lesions may appear near the genitals or rectum. Grayish-white mucous-patch sores may also appear near the mouth, throat or cervix. These symptoms will also clear up without treatment, thus leaving an individual quietly infected for the "Latent Stage."
- The Latent Stage develops roughly 2 to 30 years after the infection. During this period obvious symptoms of syphilis may not occur. Occasionally there may be recurrences of the secondary stage, along with the infectious skin disorders, but otherwise, the only way infection will be detected is by blood test.
- In the final Late Stage, tumors and bumps may develop on and damage organs. Nervous system disorders may occur and blood vessels may be injured with severe consequences such as insanity or death.

In general, regular use of latex condoms for sex (including oral and anal sex) will reduce the probability of transferring syphilis, however it will not protect an individual from contact with infectious lesions on other parts of a partner's body (e.g., on the hands, feet or mouth, etc.) For oral sex on women, you can reduce the risk of transmission by spreading kitchen plastic wrap over her vagina or anus (rimming). However, the only way to completely avoid disease transmission under these circumstances is to avoid contact completely! If you think you may have come in contact with a carrier see your doctor immediately for testing!

GONORRHEA

Like Syphilis, Gonorrhea is caused by a curable bacterium (Neisseria Gonorrhoeae). It is spread through sexual contact. Additionally, it can be spread by pregnant women to their children during the birthing process as babies pass through the birthing canal. The application of silver nitrate to the eyes of newborn babies largely reduces transmission at this mucous membrane infection site. For adults, the common infection sites are the genitalia, the mouth/throat, the rectum, and the cervix.

Untreated, in the form of Pelvic Inflammatory Disease, the disease can spread into the uterus and fallopian tubes, resulting in sterility for women and tubal (ectopic) pregnancy. For adults in general, it can additionally spread through the blood stream impacting the joints, heart valves, or the brain.

Symptoms

Symptoms may be mild in the beginning and typically appear 2 to 10 days after the sexual contact. Some individuals may not show symptoms for several months. For women initial symptoms may include a yellowish or bloody discharge from the vagina and possibly a burning sensation while urinating. Some will experience bleeding during vaginal intercourse. Approximately 80% of women will have no symptoms whatsoever and become potential unconscious spreaders of the disease. In contrast, roughly 85-90% of men will experience symptoms of painful urination and/or a yellowish-white penis discharge. These symptoms are a clear signal to see your doctor!

Although embarrassing, it is then necessary to seek out your sexual contacts and warn them that they must be tested for the disease.

Risk Reduction

Risk of spreading disease will, once again, be reduced through the use of latex condoms on men (they make condoms for women too), or the use of kitchen wrap as a barrier for performing oral sex on women. The efficacy of these barriers will be lost if body fluids are injudiciously allowed to touch the wrong side of the condom or plastic wrap.

CHLAMYDIA

Chlamydia is another bacteria-based (Chlamydia Trachomatis) infectious disease with symptoms similar to those of Gonorrhea. Both men and women may experience a burning sensation while urinating or experience unusual discharges. This may be a mild and temporary symptom. Women may additionally feel pain in the lower belly, bleeding between periods or pain during sex. However, the majority of people with this disease will experience no symptoms. This makes it quite dangerous since it can result in sterilizing infections inside the fallopian tubes or lead to tubal pregnancies. Men may also become unable to father children.

The good thing is that Chlamydia is generally easy to treat. Since symptoms will not usually appear, it is important that individuals having unprotected sex get tested for this disease on an annual basis. If you should test positive for this disease, immediately inform your sexual partners so that they too may be treated, whether or not they are showing symptoms! Risk reduction for this disease would be similar to that for Gonorrhea.

TRICHOMONIASIS

Trichomoniasis (Trich) is a common and curable STD that is caused by a parasitic protozoan (Trichomonas Vaginalis.) Infection sites for this parasite are typically the vagina for a woman and the urethra for a man. Symptoms of the infection are generally an inflammation of the infection site. This inflammation is usually so mild in men as to be unnoticeable, but may include an irritant burning sensation when urinating or mild discharge. For women the protozoan may cause a yellowish-green vaginal discharge combined with a noticeable odor. It may also result in irritation during urination and intercourse and possibly lower abdominal pains in limited cases. Symptoms take about a week before being noticed and may continue until about a month after the infection. Transmission of this parasite is usually between men and women or women and women but rarely between men. The diagnosis of the disease will require lab testing from your doctor.

Besides spreading it to other partners, the primary danger of Trich is that the resulting inflammation will make individuals (particularly women) more susceptible to infection by other STDs such as HIV.

To cure Trich requires the one-time oral application of a specific drug. However it requires that all partners be treated at the same time. Otherwise the untreated individual will continue to re-infect the other partner.

HEPATITIS B

Hepatitis B is a highly infectious viral disease that attacks the liver. Some individuals receive mild infections that go away after a short period of time while others become lifetime carriers and become a danger to their sexual partners and others. These carriers may develop and spread liver diseases such as cirrhosis of the liver which scars the liver or liver cancer.

Hepatitis B can spread in an unusual number of ways. It spreads through:

- Body fluids—such as semen, blood, saliva, vaginal fluids. The fact that it can be spread through saliva means that a Hepatitis B carrier must avoid more common forms of greeting such as kissing one's friends. These fluids can enter through mucous membranes or simply cuts or sores in the skin. In addition, the concentration of the virus in body fluids is high, making transmission more likely than, say HIV.
- Sexual activities—such as traditional, oral or anal sex.
- Sharing needles—for drug use, medicinal reasons, tattooing, ear piercing, etc.
- Sharing personal items—such as razors, toothbrushes, tongue depressors, unwashed silverware, etc.

Many individuals who catch Hepatitis B will show no symptoms. However for those who do, symptoms can include:

- Tiredness or they become very sick and lose workplace time.
- Skin or eyes becoming yellow (jaundice).

- Nausea.
- Dark-colored Urine

The best way to avoid this disease is to become vaccinated against it. The vaccine is a series of three shots given over a period of time. It is much easier to deal with the disease through prevention instead of waiting until you've caught it.

For those who have not been vaccinated, condoms should always be used. In addition, for any situations in which the mouth may spread or receive infections, a barrier such as plastic wrap or specially designed consumer oral product barriers should be used to reduce the possibility of transmitting the disease.

Currently there is no medical cure for this disease once you have it. A doctor may prescribe certain diets to treat an infected individual, however it will not eliminate the disease.

Should you find yourself living with an infected individual you should immediately go to your doctor and initiate the vaccination process as a protective measure.

HERPES

Now this is an interesting disease caused by the herpes simplex virus. This virus can affect people as cold sores and fever blisters (oral herpes), and it is estimated that roughly 80% of the adult U.S. population has this form. And it can additionally affect people as genital herpes, and an estimated 25% of U.S. adults have this form, although many are unaware due to the mildness of their cases. It comes in two related viral types, herpes simplex 1 (HSV-1) and herpes simplex 2 (HSV-2), both of which can cause cold sores or genital herpes, however usually HSV-1 causes cold sores and usually HSV-2 causes genital herpes.

Regardless of type, the disease is most infectious when the sores are open or "weeping." Particularly vulnerable areas to infection include the mucous membranes of the eyes, vagina, mouth, anus and urethra. Cuts in the skin or sores will also provide vulnerabilities. Obviously individuals with cold sores or fever blisters should not be kissing their friends. Individuals with genital herpes symptoms should not be having sex.

Initially the immune system is not well built up and so the first the first time a person catches the disease is likely to result in the most extreme reaction that the person will experience from it.

First outbreak symptoms for genital herpes usually show up within two weeks of the infection and may include:

- Blisters, open sores or pimples that are scab-like in character and may result in an uncomfortable itching on the penis, vulva, anus, pubis, thigh, buttocks, and so forth.
- Painful urination due to sores in the urethra.
- Fever.
- Swollen lymph glands near the groin.
- May not heal for 1-2 months.
- May be so minor as to be unnoticeable.

Those individuals who experience a painful initial outbreak will tend to have more obvious recurring outbreaks throughout the year. Symptoms of recurring episodes may show up as above or may appear as anomalies in the skin such as rashes, bumps, blisters or other sore-like structures. The time for these outbreaks to heal should be roughly half of the healing time for the initial outbreak.

Some individuals may never have an outbreak and may simply carry the disease. Some individuals will experience mild outbreaks and never realize that they have the disease, presuming that the irritation is due to some other cause. This is particularly a problem since they will be less likely to be concerned for their partners.

For those individuals who experience recurrences, there is a "prodrome" period beforehand that may signal the onset of the episode a day or two prior. Typical symptoms at that time would be an itching in the area where the lesions are likely to develop. In addition there may be pains in the lower back or pelvic area. From the first signal, an individual should cease all sexual activity until the complete episode has passed.

Transmittal of herpes occurs through skin to skin contact of infectious lesions, including contact of a non-sexual nature. Thus it is possible to spread the disease through simple kissing, through oral sex, through traditional, or through anal sex. Any situation that might involve touching an area that contains an outbreak of lesions can pass the disease.

The possibility of disease transmission can be decreased by:

- Abstaining from sex with your partner from the time an episode is first signaled by the prodrome until all symptoms of the outbreak have passed. During these periods the disease is most infectious. The most likely period during which herpes will be spread is during the prodrome at which time symptoms are less noticeable. Of course some people may never have any or recognize their symptoms!
- Use of latex condoms at all times between episodes. Of course this will only avoid passing the disease at locations covered by the condom. Nonetheless it is an important course of action when intimate contact is to occur. Oral barriers such as plastic wrap or commercial products should also be used when applicable.
- Make sure your partner knows of the danger and is prudently careful to avoid contact during infectious periods.
- Washing hands frequently after using the toilet,
- Washing hands before touching eyes or contact lenses,

Although this disease is not a danger to your health, it can be unpleasant, and will likely make you a social pariah if you spread it to someone else!

HPV/Genital Warts

HPV (human papillomavirus) is a sexually transmitted disease that will infect roughly 75% of the sexually active population at some point in their lifetimes. Usually these viral infections will be harmless. Some strains of the virus will cause the growth of genital warts after the infection. On a woman they may appear on the vulva, in the vagina, and on the cervix. On a man they may appear on the penis, or near the anus or scrotum. The warts can appear weeks, months or years later, or not at all. Since the appearance of symptoms may occur long after the original infection, they may not have been spread by an individual's current sexual partner.

The danger of HPV is that recent research has correlated it with the possible future development of cervical cancer for women, and anal or penile cancer for men. The danger is greater for individuals who continue to have symptoms (i.e, warts) after a number of years. This necessitates an ongoing screening process to make sure that any cancer that might result is caught in its early stage. For women, this means having a periodic "pap smear" test. Since many women will not know they have ever had HPV, it's important that all adult women engage in this screening process.

HPV is spread via skin to skin touch during traditional, anal, and occasionally oral sex. The warts themselves tend to be infectious and should not be squeezed or irritated. If large enough to be visible they can be removed medically, however the underlying virus may never leave an individual's body.

Sexually Transmitted Disease Risk Assessment

Abstinence is the safest method of avoiding sexually transmitted diseases. If you can follow this approach stop here. Otherwise read on.

For a man on the way up, a strategy of sexual encounters that is limited to careful mutual masturbation (make sure there are no cuts, sores, hangnails, scratches, etc., on your hands) quickly followed by a soap and water hand cleansing will reduce much of the risk from HIV/AIDS. *[For an even safer approach, wear latex gloves and use a commercial water-based lubricant while masturbating each other.]* Of course if you masturbate your partner and then use your own hand on yourself, you have just spread some of her body fluids onto your thingy! Don't make this error! Make sure no body fluids can be exchanged from your hand to any other part of your body. Remember, there are no guarantees of safety and it is a fatal disease.

This strategy may be less effective against syphilis, gonorrhea, chlamydia, HPV/genital warts or herpes, since a man's hand may come into contact with infectious lesions or body fluids that contain higher concentrations of the disease that may inadvertently be wiped in the eyes or spread to other mucous membranes. *[That latex glove is beginning to look good!]* Nonetheless, a thorough washing of one's hands immediately after such an encounter will reduce the possibility. Although they can be serious, when detected early, syphilis, gonorrhea and Chlamydia are curable without permanent damage. So a smart strategy for a man on the way up is to make time for an annual STD medical checkup to ensure that his health is not at risk, both for himself and his partner(s). This is even more important since carriers of these other diseases make themselves more vulnerable to infection by HIV/AIDS as a result of the lesions and inflammations that result.

HPV in some form is caught by most of the adult population at some point and should not be considered a high risk disease (otherwise by definition most of us have one). Monitoring is important however, especially for individuals who show continuing symptoms over a number of years (i.e., warts). Regardless of whether symptoms are evident or not, for women, a "pap" test should be a regular part of her medical exam regime to ensure that cervical cancer does not become a risk.

Trichomoniasis is not a particularly dangerous disease on its own. It has its irritations but is curable. Like the other diseases, it increases vulnerability to HIV and will not be easily identified in some individuals who will be unaware they have any condition at all.

Herpes is something of a wild card. It is not curable. It is not dangerous. However having it requires you to alter your social life to ensure you do not spread it inadvertently. Obviously if you see any kinds of lesions or sores (herpes or other) near a partner's private parts "stay away." There can be periods where they will not be visible however. This is a definite risk. As noted above, it is estimated that roughly 25% of the adult population has genital herpes. That tells you that it gets around and your odds are not good.

The risk assessment of Hepatitis B is that it is out there and infectious. It can be transmitted by a kiss in addition to normal sexual activity. In bad cases it can lead to fatal liver conditions. There is no excuse not to get vaccinated for this disease unless you wish to play unnecessary odds. A man on the way up will do himself a favor and get vaccinated. This is generally considered to be a safe three-part vaccination (check with your doctor of course.)

Remember, for a man on the way up, paranoia is a good thing.

www.ingramcontent.com/pod-product-compliance
Lightning Source LLC
Chambersburg PA
CBHW032125090426
42743CB00007B/471